ON THE TRAMS

Plummer's

ON THE TRAMS

Dennis Gill

Drawings by Basil Sellars

By the same author
Tramcar Treasury
Transport Treasures of Trafford Park

ISBN 0 9511458 0 0

First published 1986 by
Dennis Gill
48 Dorrington Road,
Cheadle Heath,
Stockport, Cheshire, SK3 0PZ

Printed and bound by
Deanprint Ltd.,
Cheadle Heath Works,
Stockport, Cheshire, SK3 0PR

For Betty, Karen,
Alison, Philip and Joanne

***Above:** A famous tramway centre—Manchester's Albert Square, with Edwardians flocking to the trams.*

***Frontispiece:** Every town's trams were distinctive in one way or another—especially in Southampton, the only town to run "domed roof" and "knifeboard" cars side by side. The domed roof cars, which also had low-wheeled trucks, were designed specially to pass under the city's mediaeval Bargate. The city was the last to build cars with knifeboard seating on the upper deck; some survived in service until 1949, and one is preserved at the National Tramway Museum at Crich.*

Contents

Preface

This is a book of unusual stories about trams. It is not a history of trams or a technical book. It is a book I hope many will find entertaining.

Mainly anecdotal, it is packed with strange tales, curious and little-known facts and colourful comments.

It's about the people and animals that rode on the trams, about the men and women who worked on them, and about the many fascinating things that have happened on trams.

What connection, for instance, did Jekyll and Hyde have with Stockport trams and how was a pedestrian shot in the leg by a tramcar in Ashton-under-Lyne?

How did a rat and conger eel hold up tramway services—and what happened when a London tram was hijacked? The answers, and lots more, can be found in these pages.

The stories have come from a variety of sources, many of them gleaned through a lifetime's interest in trams. One or two of them may be well-known, but many are brand new and previously unpublished.

In seeking out fresh material I have been considerably helped by retired tramway employees and fellow tram enthusiasts (in particular, Geoffrey Claydon of London and Terence Goulding of Bolton), and also by members of the public who wrote to me after reading my first book, "Tramcar Treasury," or in response to my letters in newspapers.

Regrettably, some of those who supplied me with information have passed away. They included two fellow enthusiasts—Hugh Nicol of Glasgow and Maurice Marshall of Stockport, both of whom had an extensive knowledge of tramway related matters. Dr. Nicol, especially, shared my interest in the extraordinary and unique, and provided me with many useful references.

Other valuable sources of information were the enthusiast magazines *Modern Tramway* and *Tramway Review,* published by the Light Rail Transit

An early example of tramway "pop" art. A Hull tram specially embellished in 1921 to celebrate the tercentenary of Andrew Marvell (1621-78) the poet and writer who became MP for Hull in 1659.

Association, and very early volumes of some of the professional transport magazines, such as *The Tramway and Light Railway World,* kindly loaned by the Greater Manchester Transport Society.

I also found some of the histories on individual tramway systems invaluable, especially "The Giant's Causeway Tramway" by J. H. McGuigan and "The Manchester Tram" by Ian Yearsley, both published in the early sixties.

I would like to express my special gratitude to ex-Guardian cartoonist Basil Sellars for his excellent drawings. His interest and his enthusiasm have been very encouraging.

My special thanks, also, to all those who kindly provided me with photographs. They are credited at the end of this book.

Finally, but certainly not least, I must record the debt I owe my wife for her constant encouragement and support. She has made helpful criticisms, assisted with proof reading and suffered uncomplainingly the inconvenience and tribulations caused by a project of this nature.

Tribute to the tram

Of all the magnificent vehicles invented in the last century, one of the most fascinating was the tramcar.

For conveying large numbers of people in towns and cities, it hasn't yet been surpassed, and it still flourishes, incorporating all the latest computerised technology, in many European towns.

Yet in Britain it is virtually extinct, and there are generations who have never enjoyed the delights of riding on a tram.

Indeed, there are some people who have no idea what a tramcar is, or what it looks like. How do you describe this vehicle that once ran on lines down the main thoroughfares of our cities and towns?

A carriage on rails pulled along by a clothes prop? A sardine tin on its side? Two date boxes, one on top of the other?

One author described it as the "high-built glittering galleon of the streets." And it is not too difficult to see why.

It had a hull which was curved and rounded, not unlike a ship's, and railings round the upper deck.

It had bulkheads, and a bell which clanged a warning in clinging suffocating fogs.

And it had a "ship's wheel." The driver stood beside it on his platform, like the captain on his bridge.

Even the wooden seating in the lower saloons ran longitudinally, like the seats round the sides of steerage saloons on small steamers.

And sticking out of the top deck on the early open-toppers was the mast—the trolley mast, on which swivelled the trolley pole to which flags were sometimes attached.

The similarity was not lost on towns like Bristol, Burnley and Blackpool, where trams were "dressed up" as ships or boats for special occasions, such as carnivals and illuminations.

There were classes of tram which even had names with seafaring connotations—Showboat, Cunarder, Dreadnought, Submarine, Boat, to mention just a few. And there were individual trams at South Shields named after liners like the Mauritania and the Monarch of Bermuda.

Unlike most sea-going vessels, however, the tram didn't have a stern. It was the same fore and aft. Confusing that, for sometimes you couldn't be sure whether it was coming or going.

When the tram reached a terminus it didn't reverse like a bus. The driver simply changed ends. There were platforms equipped with controls at both ends, and the driver stood on the platform turning two brass handles. One worked the controller, the magical box of tricks which set the car in motion; the other manipulated a brake.

There were also stairs at both ends. It meant trams didn't need a safety exit. A comforting thought if ever there was an accident or a fire.

If you didn't like travelling forwards you could travel backwards. The choice was yours. All you had to do was turn over the seat back-rests.

Conductors flipped them over like a deck of cards every time the terminus was reached. They made a loud clacking noise, and children were tempted to do it for fun.

At the terminus it was also the conductor's duty to swing the trolley pole round. The pole swivelled on the roof of the tram and sloped skywards, pressing against glistening electrical wires suspended directly above the tracks. Electricity shot down the poles and passed through the controllers to the motors, which kept the wheels turning.

As it moved along the wire, the pole made a sizzling sound, like juicy sausages frying in a pan. And at complicated junctions it gave out bright iridescent flashes, sending sparks cascading to the ground like silver fountains at a firework display.

To those who didn't know what the sparking meant it was jokingly explained: "Why, when the conductor sees that he knows that all's right at the head office."

Without the trolley pole, of course, the tram was stranded. As helplessly as a whale on a mud bank.

Trams came in all sorts of shapes and sizes: eight-wheel and four-wheel; double deck and single deck; all enclosed and open on top. There were single deckers shaped like toast racks, and special breeds with cabs which stuck out at each end.

There were some with vestibules and some without, and others with balconies. There were some with open staircases and some with reversed stairs. A few had two sets of stairs at each end, and there were even some with two sets of stairs in the middle.

All the trams were solidly constructed, with hearts of oak, like seventeenth century warships.

Craftsmen built them. It was reflected in the carved mouldings, in the bevelled, fluted and beaded pillars and frames, and in the bird's-eye maple ceilings and stained glass window ventilators.

Ship of the road. A tram in sea-going disguise at Burnley on a fund-raising mission for the local hospital.

They were constructed with loving care and pride. If only the same could be said for the mass-produced vehicles of today.

You wondered why the trams didn't go on for ever. Somehow they seemed permanent—like the town hall. They belonged to the people. They gave towns and cities character.

This was especially true at Glasgow, where they were as famous as the cable cars are in San Francisco. The trams dominated Glasgow and there were gleaming lines down the centre of all its major thoroughfares.

Other road users, of course, didn't like the tram rails in the centre of the road. They would have preferred them to be laid elsewhere—on viaducts, in subways or on median strips.

But when the tramways were first laid it never occurred to municipalities to put them anywhere else but in the centre of the road. Tunnels exclusively for trams would have solved a lot of problems, however. But where would the fun have been in riding on top of a car in a dark tunnel?

Trams saved ratepayers quite large sums in road costs. For tram operators maintained that section of road where their tracks were laid. The tram tracks usually had the best surface, and other road users drove along them, although they paid not a penny towards maintenance costs.

The tram tracks divided traffic into orderly lanes. They were also landmarks, for where the shiny metals started and ended that was where towns started and ended.

They were also a big help when you lost your bearings, especially in foggy weather. ''Follow the tram lines,'' they said. ''You can't go wrong.''

You knew when a tram was coming. That was another pleasing aspect. It didn't slink up on you unannounced. You could hear it half a mile away—and get to the stop in time to catch it.

The drone of the tram's electric motors was reassuring—the most recognisable and musical of city sounds. Not an assault on the ears, like the roar of motorbikes. Some even found it soporific. It suggested dedication and concern, and the traveller was grateful.

The benefits of the clean, brilliantly-lit and fast electric trams were apparent from the moment they burst on the city scene in the 1890s.

Crowds flocked to ride on them and there wasn't a town where they were not packed on opening day.

''No one gets off and no one can get on. Full cars reach the terminus, but no one alights and the whole cargo goes back again,'' reported one newspaper at the opening of Kirkcaldy's tramway system.

The Halifax Building Society celebrated 50 years in the City of London with this mock tram in the 1982 Lord Mayor's Show.

"We now have graceful and pretty vehicles, beautifully illuminated at night, moving along the roads with greater speed, with unprecedented smoothness and noiselessness, and for one third the fare," said a newspaper in Chester.

"One really wonders how we got on so long without them," wrote the *Hamilton Advertiser.*

H. G. Wells, the famous science fiction novelist, saw tramways as "beautiful things." He said there was no reason why they shouldn't be as gracious as Nature made the stems of her plants and the joints of her animals.

He could see tramways running in ideal settings, spreading over the land in fine reticulations and making a real contribution to the advancement of our civilisation.

In fact, by 1910 the number of trams running in Britain had increased to 12,000, reaching a maximum of 15,000 by 1926 with vast networks of lines in the large industrial centres.

Trams revolutionised city travel and city life. They made it possible for workers to live farther out in the suburbs. They gave better roads. They played a big part in developing electricity supplies, providing the means for the construction of more power stations.

They relieved unemployment by creating a new transport industry with a whole range of associated electrical industries. They brought improved working conditions, pay and welfare for transport employees.

They contributed enormously to leisure activities, bringing bigger crowds to theatres and football matches, and taking thousands of children on outings and picnics. And they helped relieve rates.

The coming of the electric tram, in fact, was almost as big a boon in the Edwardian era as railways were at the beginning of the Victorian era.

But as quickly as they came the trams fell out of favour. By 1930 they had started to disappear. The fell victim to pirate buses and unfair competition, political manoeuvring, poor management, inadequate technical knowledge, lack of development, meagre finances, poor co-operation and outdated legislation which imposed intolerable burdens.

Nor were they helped by the press, which was generally hostile, misleading, and pitifully parochial and insular.

The trams were given a quick execution in some towns; and suffered a lingering and painful demise in the largest cities.

In Coventry and Bristol they were blasted out of existence by Hitler's bombs.

But what funerals they gave the trams. People turned out in their thousands to pay their last respects. You might have thought it was a king or a popular hero they were burying.

In Glasgow three quarters of a million people lined the streets in 1962 to see the last tram procession—the biggest crowds since VE Day. The people clung to their trams to the very last.

My word

SMART THINKING

Reverse trams and you get—smart.

IN ONE WORD

Sweden has the longest tramway word in the world—93 letters long. It is: SPARVAGSAKTIEBOLAGSSKENSMUTSSKJUTAREFACKFORE-NINGSPERSONALBEKLADNADSMAGASINSFORRADSFORVALTA-REN, which means "The manager of the depot for the supply of uniforms to the personnel of the track cleaners' union of the street railway company."

JEKYLL AND HYDE

In the early days of Stockport tramways, cars displayed bye-laws and regulations signed by Jekyll and Hyde. Jekyll was the name of the Board of Trade assistant secretary and Hyde was Stockport's town clerk.

UNIFORM MISTAKE

There were no smart uniforms for staff of the Sunderland District tramways on opening day in 1905. Instead of being sent to the company's head office at Philadelphia in Durham, the uniforms had been sent by mistake to Philadelphia in America.

MANCHESTER SPIT CANAL

The joke was missed by advertising agents, but not by passengers when "Use the Ship Canal" stickers appeared beneath "Do not spit" signs on Manchester trams.

SPECIAL NAME

A trams horse at Worcester was called Telegraph—because it arrived the day the tramway office was connected to the central exchange.

DELIVERED ON BOARD

A nun gave birth in a Naples tram in 1925, and the Royal Canadian Navy had an officer called Trammy Fee—so called because he had been born in a tram.

Big red bogie cars dominated Manchester's central streets. This busy scene is outside the Daily Express offices in Great Ancoats Street.

Hold tight

A sticky situation developed on London tramways in 1913. It happened when a London County Council tramcar collided with a van carrying stationery to a printing company.

The van fell on its side and casks of glue fell out, spilling their contents all over the tracks.

Three conductors and a policeman who tried to right the van were covered with glue. Stationery stuck to their clothes and they were soon in difficulties. Their subsequent attempts to free themselves brought howls of laughter from an ever-growing crowd of onlookers.

When a tramway official who had been taking down details of the accident attempted to move away he found that the soles of his boots were stuck to the wooden paving. Two conductors rushed to his aid, and after a great deal of tugging released him, but one of his boots stayed stuck to the pavement.

Hardly a day passed without some amusing incident like this occurring on tramcars, especially in the twenties, when the number of tramcars on the streets was at its peak.

Stockport tram driver Norman May had a fund of tales spanning his 50-year career. He recalled how in a pea-soup fog a cyclist followed a tramcar into the centre of Stockport with unexpected results.

"What the cyclist didn't know was that the tram was going to the depot in Mersey Square," said Mr. May. "He followed it straight into the sheds and fell, bicycle and all, down a repair pit."

Mr. May also recalled an amusing incident when trams were stopped by a power failure. Apparently, with their vehicle immobile, the crew of one tram sat down on its rear fender. Unfortunately, the driver had left the controller handle on the first power notch, and when the electricity was restored, the tram moved off on its own, leaving both men sitting in the middle of the road.

Inspectors, too, have had their off moments. Like the one at Birmingham who took matters into his own hands when a driver refused to take his tram down hilly Warstone Lane. The driver was reluctant to proceed because he was not satisfied that his magnetic track brake was working correctly.

"There's nothing wrong with the brake," insisted the inspector. And to prove it he took the car down the hill himself. The brake failed to work, and the tramcar overturned at the bottom of the hill, realising the driver's worst fears and bringing forth some four-letter words from the inspector, only one of which rhymed with tram.

Crews and officials were rarely short of choice expressions, especially at moments like this. But their comments and dry wit were not always appreciated by passengers.

Visitors to London who asked what they should get for the "Elephant" didn't take kindly to being told "Buns!" The "Elephant" they were enquiring about was the "Elephant and Castle" public house at an important South London tramway junction.

There was the same sort of witticism in Manchester. When asked if their tram was going to the Opera House, conductors would often be tempted to reply: "It docsn't sing!"

A Mancunian unable to board a tram in Piccadilly because it was full asked the conductor: "How long will the next one be?" The conductor stuck his head outside the tram, looked up and down and said: "Same length as this one."

And in Liverpool, a favourite reply to visitors asking "Do you stop at the Adelphi Hotel?" was "No sir, not on the wages they pay me!"

There was also humour which resulted directly from misunderstandings. Like the time some American airmen travelling on a Liverpool tramcar stood to attention when the conductor shouted out "Stanhope Street." They all thought he had commanded "Stand up straight!"

Like the time a music lover in New York asked for the whereabouts of Leopold Stokowski, the famous conductor. The music lover was advised to try the car barns.

And like the time the depot foreman at Wallasey asked what colour he should paint the trams. "See Greene," he was told, Greene being the name of the general manager. So that is what the foreman did—he painted the cars "sea green."

In Cornwall, a woman who went down the front-end stairs of a Camborne tramcar was politely asked by the driver to "go down the other way." The driver meant her to go down the stairs at the other end, but she climbed back up the stairs, and came down again—backwards.

For some women, climbing up and down tramcar stairs was by no means a laughing matter. In Stockport, a drunken 16-stone woman slipped as she came down the spiral staircase. Her legs shot out through the railings on each side, leaving her lying on her back, straddled across the stairs, unable to move up or down.

"Their subsequent attempts to free themselves brought howls of laughter from an ever-growing crowd . . ."

Basil Sellars

She presented a very embarrassing spectacle to conductor John Robert Pickering Jones and his driver, who had an agonising time freeing her.

They were lucky she wasn't as heavy as one of Chatham's tram drivers. He weighed 22 stones and never stood on the top of a tramcar throughout his long driving career. The staircases were too narrow for him to climb.

It wasn't only while climbing down stairs that passengers got themselves into trouble. Alighting from trams presented problems, too. A woman who stepped off a London car was left spinning—literally. The braid in her dress had got caught in the step. As the tram set off it left her spinning on her heels as yard after yard of the braid unwound from her skirt.

In Liverpool, automatically-operated track points ensnared a woman as she crossed in front of a tramcar. The point snapped shut like a vice, trapping the stiletto heel of her shoe. The surprised lady slipped her foot out of the shoe and broke into a run, leaving the shoe in the track.

There have been other occasions when women's fashion has proved hazardous to tram passengers. One of the biggest menaces was hat pins, and there were many complaints from passengers scratched and cut by them.

In Hamburg and Munich, women wearing hat pins were told that they could only ride on the trams if they bought a protective cork or wooden tip from the conductor for a small sum.

In Manchester, a victim writing to the local paper said he had been marked for life on his nose by one of "those attrocious stiletto-like weapons." He went on: "It occurred through the woman—one of the most fidgety of creatures—suddenly turning to gaze out of the window."

A Manchester conductor caught under the eye by a pin belonging to a lady squeezing past him was so badly gashed that the blood flowed freely down his coat.

These problems, though, were fairly straightforward compared to the one facing a woman bruised in a tram accident abroad. The accident, according to one newspaper, led to her becoming a nymphomaniac, giving her a craving for "emotional substance" and leading to her taking 100 lovers in five years.

Some of the most unexpected accidents on tramways were caused by the rope attached to the trolley pole. A woman standing on the top deck of an open-top Stalybridge tramcar was lassoed by the trailing rope of a tramcar passing in the opposite direction and thrown to the ground. Miraculously, she suffered only slight concussion and recovered shortly afterwards.

At Carlisle, a conductor hauled down the trolley boom so that his driver could coast their tram past a section of wire under repair. Unfortunately, when he came to put the boom back on the wire, while the car was still moving, the trolley rope looped itself round one of the projecting bracket arms supporting the overhead wire.

The rope tightened round his hand and he was hauled five feet from the ground. He was saved by a following motorist who, having seen his predicament, ran his vehicle under him to break his fall.

There were occasions when trams lost power through becoming grounded, especially on rarely-used sections of track. If the wheels came to rest on dirt or sand lodged in the grooved rails, the return circuit for the current (via the rails) would be broken and the car would become open-circuited.

It often had the effect of giving an electric shock to anybody who touched the handrails or metal parts of the tram. When this happened, crews usually pulled the trolley boom off the wire to prevent passengers from getting hurt.

On one dark night a driver on a north eastern system drove his tram onto some dirt-covered track at a terminus. Not realising the car was grounded, the conductor went behind the car to relieve himself, as there were no toilets nearby, and received an electric shock which sent him leaping high in the air and left him walking strangely for days afterwards.

The fear of getting electric shocks from trams and rails was a matter of some public concern when tramways first opened.

In Northern Ireland two men took their trousers down and sat on an electric third rail to prove the current it carried did not give fatal shocks.

The two gentlemen were tramway pioneers William Traill and Dr. Edward Hopkinson, and they performed this extraordinary act during the official inspection of the Giant's Causeway line at Portrush—the second electric tramway to open in the British Isles.

The third rail carried current at 250 volts and the two men gave their impromptu demonstration when asked if it would be dangerous for a beggar with torn trousers to sit on the line.

Mr. Traill said that one benefit of feeling the current was that it cured rheumatism and he quoted the case of one sufferer who was able to open his hand after touching the rail a number of times.

Later, however, a notice appeared on the tramway which said: "Do not touch the naked conductor running alongside the track." As can be imagined, a lot of ribald comments were made about that!

Conductors and drivers were given instruction on how to deal with persons rendered insensible by electric shock and how to deal with loose electric wires when there was an accident.

They were also instructed on how to make simple repairs and were advised to wear protective clothing when examining electrical parts and motors, and not to place themselves in a position where a jerk would pitch them into the vehicle's mechanism.

In wartime Manchester, a driver was seen to make a very simple repair with a piece of string. His tram had suffered from iron hiccups for a mile and a half after leaving town, so it was no surprise to the passengers when it died in its tracks.

After a lot of curses and clankings, the driver flung back the saloon

"Saved by a following motorist . . ."

door and asked if anybody had some string. A woman produced a piece, and with help from a passing driver the tram was soon on its way, lame and halting, but sustained by conjecture and pride.

Said a passenger: "We felt a distinct distant relationship with the pilot who successfully reaches home with a shot-up plane."

At Gateshead, when smoke started to issue from a tram, the driver lifted up the floor boards and leant into one of the car's bogies, virtually disappearing from sight. All that passengers could see were his legs sticking out in the saloon. Somehow he stopped the smoke, and the car proceeded cautiously on its way.

Not so handy was the conductor of a tramcar at Liege in Belgium. When the current-collecting wheel at the end of the trolley boom fell into the street, he picked it up and asked his driver what he should do with it. It was a silly question, for obviously it had to go back on the trolley boom, otherwise the tram would remain immobile.

The driver replied sarcastically: "Put it down at the side of the road. We'll pick it up on our way back!"

The tramway

Along the highways
And over the hills,
Down in the valleys
Past tall darkened mills,
Through squares full of people
On market day,
Past theatre and steeple,
You would find the tramway.

Where steel rails were laid
And wires above hung,
Where cheap fares were paid
And two bells rung,
Where car after car would glide
From dawn till night each day,
Packed tight with people inside,
You would find the tramway.

—Author

Fizz please! Bars designed to look like trams at the Lynstead Private Hotel in Blackpool (above) with proprietors Jim and Doreen Shearer, and (below) at the No. 53 public house in Manchester, on the city's former No. 53 tram route.

Cheers!

BUBBLE TROUBLE

Banquets were held to celebrate the opening of most tramways—but after Stockport's celebratory feast there was uproar when it was discovered that 155 guests had consumed 154 bottles of champagne.

CHAMPAGNE BREAKFAST

The King of Siam opened the Bangkok tramways in 1905 by tightening the last fish bolt on the line and switching on the current. But the first tram on the system carried Brahmin and Buddhist monks as the king went for a champagne breakfast before touring the system himself.

RAIL ALE

Beer was poured in the rails in front of the first car at the opening of a new Hannover tram route in 1955—and a good time was had by all.

Six beer barrels unloaded from a brewer's dray blocked the path of a trial car on the Rhondda tramways. Local dignitaries on board the tram were asked if they were "good beer shifters."

FIRST-CLASS COFFEE

Coffee was served in the first-class sections of Belem (Para) tramcars in Brazil. First-class passengers had to wear a hat and jacket.

PENNY PLAIN

Penny chocolate machines were installed on the upper decks of London trams based at Hammersmith.

FOOD FOR THOUGHT

Nearly half a million parcels were carried by Black Country trams in 1915, including potatoes in 10-ton loads, margarine, cocoa, foodstuffs and tobacco in cases.

MILKY WAY

Milk was carried by Halifax tramways. It cost £1 a month to send about 30 gallons a day three stages. Milk churns were also carried by Leeds trams and on the Dudley to Stourbridge tramway.

Just the ticket

FLICKER TICKET

A sixpenny return ticket bought on a Camborne tram in Cornwall also gave admission to a local film show.

ALL DAY AT WILL

A Highgate man set a record for tram riding in 1930. He travelled 175 miles on the London County Council tramways with a shilling-all-day ride-at-will ticket. Starting at 5.22 a.m., he journeyed on 31 trams, finishing at 2.05 a.m. the next day. At the ordinary single fares his journeys would have cost him 9s 2d. His ticket expired at 3 a.m.

PENNY DIFFERENT

It cost twopence to ride on a tram up Hastings High Street, but only a penny to ride down it.

STOCK SHOCK

Salford tramways had to borrow tickets from neighbouring systems in 1928 when fire destroyed most of the ticket stocks at the Frederick Road offices.

GOLD BAR

Ipswich tramcars carried a notice which said: "Gold coins will not be accepted in payment of fare."

AT CROSS PURPOSES

Several patriotic Oslo tram conductors were arrested during the second world war for handing tickets to passengers with the sun cross—the Quisling sign—upside down.

FARE AFFAIR

The introduction of tram tickets in Leeds met with stiff opposition when nearly 100 conductors had sums deducted from their pay packets because their receipts did not tally with the numbers of tickets issued.

At the former Whitehall steam tram terminus in Darwen can be found this mural depicting the town's tramway system. In the foreground is a section of preserved steam tramway track.

Brilliant flashes

"I purposely followed a tram from Old Market to St. George's fountain and counted no less than 58 brilliant flashes. Multiply this by, say, 40 trams and you have 2,500 flashes every 15 minutes! Should not the trams be stopped on the air-raid signal being given?"

—Anxious Bristolian during the second world war

"Well, bedad, I've seen tramcars pulled by 'osses and driven by steam, but this is the first toime I iver saw one pulled by a fishing rod!"

—Irish labourer, seeing an electric tram for the first time

"I am giving the conductors a lecture in the morning, teaching them how to move about a crowded car without tumbling into the laps of ladies."

—Peterborough tramways manager on opening day

"If you saw Syd's wife you'd understand why he loved trams."

—Tram conductor talking about his mate

"I would sooner have a pin-up of a Middleton bogie tramcar than one of a film star, any day."

—Roy Brook, author of "Tramways of Huddersfield"

"As against an electric car, the motorbus has about the relative value of a perambulator."

—Sir Clifton Robinson, managing director, London United Tramways

"Wasn't greeted with open arms . . ."

Animal antics

Stockport tram conductors turned a blind eye whenever Kruger Rogerson boarded a car unescorted.

For Kruger was a mongrel dog with amazing navigational powers, who knew which trams to catch to take him to his destination.

He was the pet of a Cheadle Heath road pavior who worked at Mottram in Longdendale.

Each morning the pavior travelled to work by tram and train, changing trams at Mersey Square, in the centre of Stockport, and boarding a train at Hyde.

Kruger always went with him, except when he overslept after a night out on the tiles.

When this happened, Kruger would set off on his own as soon as he woke up, catch all the necessary connections, and eventually join up with his master in Mottram.

This remarkable dog, who was able to tell where a tram was going, is one of many animals who over the years have contributed to tramway folklore. Not everybody's pet, however, was made as welcome on the trams as Kruger.

One that certainly wasn't greeted with open arms was the bear which climbed to the top deck of a Lowestoft tram before the first world war. It was a dancing bear, but nobody stayed up top long enough to see how well it could jig to tunes played on a concertina by its master.

Needless to say, the crew responsible for allowing it on board had some explaining to do back at the depot, and from then onwards bears were strictly banned from riding on the trams.

In Manchester there was trouble when a passenger refused to pay twopence for the hen he took on a car in Oldham Street.

"It's alive, so it has to be paid for," insisted the conductor.

"I'll soon put that right," snorted the passenger, and he wrung the bird's neck.

Women screamed and fighting broke out, which led to the owner of the hen being fined for disorderly conduct.

Strangely enough, twopence was all that was charged by Lowestoft tramways for carrying a baby elephant a couple of miles on one of its cars.

But before the baby elephant, which belonged to a visiting circus, was allowed on board, the floor of the tram had to be specially strengthened.

When an elephant was taken for a ride on one of the monorail cars at Wuppertal in Germany, the floor proved inadequate and the unfortunate creature fell into the river Wupper below.

The reluctance of some tramway operators to carry animals was understandable. They claimed that if animals were allowed on the cars they might annoy, frighten or injure their passengers. Also, they could present awkward problems if they escaped, as Coventry conductor Harry Wilkinson discovered when a ragamuffin boarded his tram one day.

The ragamuffin, known as a "tatter" in Coventry parlance, was carrying a goose and attempted to enter the lower saloon. Knowing that geese could give a nasty nip if aroused, Mr. Wilkinson ordered the fellow upstairs and told him to sit on the curved balcony seat.

As the tram approached Bedworth, it passed under a railway bridge which amplified the swish of the trolley. The noise frightened the goose and caused it to take flight. The poor owner dashed downstairs, shouting: "Stop the tram, my goose has gone!"

Mr. Wilkinson recalled: "Although there were fields on either side of the road, the bird was nowhere to be seen. After about five minutes I told the tatter that we would have to continue with the journey and leave him to search on his own.

"Tuppeny, please!"

"Dislodged the bird by giving it a nudge with the trolley pole . . ."

"Walking back to the tram, I glanced up and saw the goose sitting on the roof. I pointed it out to the tatter and he started to bombard it with stones and clods of earth in an effort to dislodge it, until I told him he was endangering passengers and tramcar alike."

Mr. Wilkinson himself eventually dislodged the bird by giving it a nudge with the trolley pole, and it flew to the ground.

Another incident involving a goose, this time a dead one, occurred on the Birmingham and Midland tramways. A man was taking the bird home for Christmas, and decided, for the sake of other passengers, to hang it outside the car. So he tied it by its neck to the upper deck railings.

When he reached his stop and got hold of the goose's neck he found to his utter astonishment that the body had dropped off. He then had to set off back down the track to find it.

The body had parted company from the head, it is believed, because of the motion of the tram in swinging in and out of countless loops on the journey to Dudley.

Although the side rails were handy for tying up dead geese and other fowl, the platform handrails were a positive hazard for goats and rams.

A lascar discovered this in Glasgow when he took a goat, his regiment's mascot, on board a tram. The goat's horns got entwined round the handrail as it was disembarking, and the tram was held up for some while as the lascar struggled to free it.

Tramcar operators also recognised that animals on the street might present problems on occasions. If a horse wasn't broken in properly, the awesome sight of an electric tram would sometimes cause it to panic and let fly with its hooves. Because of this, drivers were instructed "to stop their cars when meeting restless horses."

A tramcar frightened a horse being broken in on the busy streets of Bolton in 1905. The horse kicked in a shop window and pranced about the streets on its rear legs.

When a woman asked the owner why he didn't break his horse in at Deane or Halliwell, where there was less traffic, he said: "There are more trams here and the horses are sooner broken."

"And the windows, too!" she promptly retorted.

In London a horse fell under the tram tracks in 1923. It hadn't noticed there was a hole in the road and fell into a 10ft-deep excavation. A crane and sling had to be brought from Hackney Depot to rescue it.

Cattle were even less enamoured with trams when coming face to face with them.

In Blackpool, a heifer charged a tram head on. The fear-crazed animal had escaped from a slaughterhouse. After ramming the tram, it headed towards the station with three police cars in pursuit and was eventually trapped in a back street.

In Manchester in 1932, an inward-bound rush-hour tram met a line of elephants nose-to-tail in Brunswick Street.

The sight of the tram was too much for one elephant and it sat down on the tracks. By the time the mahout in charge had persuaded the offender to get up and move on a long line of trams had built up.

"When I arrived at the office half an hour late and told my boss that the trams had been held up by an elephant he would not believe me," said one worker.

The electric tramway service on the Phoenix Park route in Dublin was brought to a standstill by similarly perverse conduct by a cow. It was being driven along the street when it lay down on the tram tracks to rest. Every effort short of violence was brought to bear on the cow, but without effect.

Ultimately ropes were fetched. Just as a tall policeman was about to give the order "Pull away," the cow rose to its feet, looked about in disdain, and calmly walked off.

Two cows blocked the path of the two special cars that made the inaugural run on Middleton's tramways on 14 April, 1902. Like the cow in Dublin, they were very stubborn, all attempts to move them failing until the cowman arrived and drove them off the track.

Trams have also been held up by a rat, bees and, incredibly, a conger eel.

The rat held up Belfast's tramway service in 1923 when it got into the high-tension switchgear at the power station and caused a short circuit. A swarm of bees stopped Maidstone's trams in 1922 when they settled on the trolley pole of a car passing down the main street, and the conger eel brought Plymouth's trams to a halt for an hour one day in July 1920 when it got into the force pump at the generating station and choked it.

Another surprising delay occurred near Fleetwood when a hare derailed a tram. The derailment occurred when the hare ran into the tram's lifeguard, causing it to drop down on the track. The hare was uninjured and ran off into the hedgerow.

Countless other animals, as well as humans, have been saved from death by tramcar lifeguards.

Commenting on the effectiveness of Tidswell's new patented lifeguard on the tramcars at Bradford, the local *Daily Argus* said in 1901: "A few days ago a too-venturesome pussy got in front of an electric car in Bolton Road, and it was threatened with an untimely end. The feline obstruction passed under the car and the brakes were promptly applied, but before a halt could be made pussy trotted out from underneath and scampered away up a side street. The apparatus had done its work."

Another lifesaver on trams were the dog gates. They hung between the bogies, one on each side of the car, and prevented dogs and other small creatures from running between the wheels and getting cut in two.

Of course, there were tramway accidents involving animals which didn't have happy endings. In January, 1904, the overhead wires at Brentford broke and fell on two horses being driven alongside the tram tracks. The wires wound round both animals and they fell to the ground, with electric shocks passing through their bodies.

One newspaper reported: "The horses were soon in their death struggles, as the wires set fire to them. Both the animals suffered terrible agony and for a long time after their struggles had ceased their bodies continued to burn, as it was found impossible to extricate them from the live wires."

Offsetting these tragedies was the typically-British compassion extended to some animals and birds by tramway operators. There was an excellent example of this at Southend-on-Sea.

Two robins had built a nest under the wrought iron stairs of a car standing on a track inside the main depot. A mechanic spotted the nest before the car was driven off, and reported it to his superior. Officials were consulted, but nobody was heartless enough to move the car, and it was withheld from service until the fledglings had flown.

It was more usual, of course, for birds to build their nests in depot rafters, rather than in trams—at much safer distances from depot cats which were constantly on the prowl.

The robins at Southend obviously fancied tramcars as much as did a Blackburn homing pigeon and Nelson, a Southampton cat with only one eye.

The pigeon was regularly taken in a basket to the Old Mother Red Cap Inn and released there, but it had distinctive homing ideas.

A *Lancashire Evening Telegraph* reader said: "It would find a convenient perch and wait for the next tram to town; riding on the safety rail if it was an open double decker; on the arm that contacted the cable if it was a single; and only taking off again a short flight from home."

Nelson the cat rode on Southampton trams between the wars, and knew where he was going and where he wanted to get off.

In the 100th issue of *Tramway Review,* Frank Dix, a former editor of the magazine, recalls his first meeting with Nelson.

"I first saw him curled up on the top-deck seat of a tram on the Shirley route. I introduced myself and he left the bare wood and sat on my knee," said Mr. Dix, who took great delight in riding on the trams of every town he visited.

He saw Nelson nearly every day after that meeting, but got the shock of his life when Nelson followed him onto a Plymouth-bound train.

"I didn't see him until he jumped into the compartment with me just as the train started," said Mr. Dix. "He came with me to Plymouth and there we rode the trams together for a whole week.

"Fortunately I was going from there to Portsmouth, so I broke my journey at Southampton and put him on a tram to find his way home. I felt a bit lonely riding the Portsmouth trams without Nelson, and I often wonder if he was still alive when the Southampton trams were scrapped and whether he deigned to ride on a bus."

A monkey found riding alone on a Bolton tram in 1906 was not as fortunate as Nelson. He was taken to the lost property office, where he led officials a pretty dance, showing some of them the sharpness of his teeth.

A sailor eventually claimed him. He grabbed the monkey by his tail, gave him a swing and had him in a cage before the onlookers could quite take in the situation.

Knowing how to handle animals is half the battle—and at Stalybridge tram depot it helped them bring home the bacon when it was most needed. For during both world wars they kept pigs in some vacant sheds at the side of the depot.

The pigs belonged to a "pig club" formed among employees of the Stalybridge, Hyde, Mossley and Dukinfield Tramways and Electricity Board—known locally as the SHMD.

Members of the club provided the capital to buy the pigs (with one pound shares in the first world war and two shilling shares in the second), contributed waste food to fatten them, and shared in the distribution of joints after the pigs had been slaughtered.

All went well until George Grundy, general manager and founder of the club, sent out slips asking members which joints they preferred. Eighty per cent wrote back saying "leg joints."

"I then had to send out further slips informing members we were killing pigs, not centipedes," recalled Mr. Grundy.

"I don't care if it does say 'Zoo' on it; they can't have it for their tea party!"

Joy ride

"Talk about the pleasure of the joywheel! Compared with the joy of a ride on the top of a Rhondda tram, the joywheel is a hopeless back number."

—Swansea reporter

"It has been estimated that in the case of a tramcar weighing six tons and running at 10 miles an hour, with operating costs at fourpence a mile, the cost of stopping the vehicle four times a mile is 0.22d. A passenger who stops such a car causes an energy expenditure of 45,000 ft/lbs, and allowing for both entering and leaving the vehicle, the amount is doubled. As only 6,600 ft/lbs are required to carry him a mile, it follows that he could have been carried over 12 miles for the same expenditure of energy. The importance of having regular stopping places will thus be seen . . ."

—Tramway and Railway World

"A bus is a vehicle—a tram is a system."

—Wingate Bett, tramway connoisseur

"As a business rider, six days a week, I much prefer trams to buses when it comes to company . . . The places where they turn left or right are clearly defined and the cyclist feels a sense of safety as he pedals alongside a swiftly moving tram such as he can never feel when a motor bus is within inches of his person."

—Editor of The Bicycle

"The secret of the tram is that not only does it need much narrower lanes than a bus, but that it has a psychological superiority over the motorist, who might ignore bus lanes but is not going to stray over the very visible lines along which a three-carriage tram might come thundering any minute."

—The Sunday Times

It took ten days in 1903 to lay this special trackwork at Leicester's Clock Tower—one of the most complicated tramway junctions in Britain.

Track record

ON THE LEVEL

There were 34 level railway crossings on the two and a half miles of tram track in Trafford Park, near Manchester—one every 122 yards.

GIGANTIC RENEWAL

The biggest tramway track renewal programme in a city occurred in Toronto between 1 September, 1921, and 31 December, 1923. Nearly 4,000 men relaid 115 miles of track, using more than eight million granite setts, 7,000 freight car loads of sand, stone and gravel, 750 freight car loads of cement, 37,500 tie rods, 274,000 tie plates, 120 intersections, 14 loops and 82 electric points. During the same period 575 new steel cars and trailers entered service.

KEEPING TRACK

When tram services ended in the Potteries in 1928, 30 miles of track were left in the streets. In 1981, more than half a century later, some 10 miles still remained intact, beneath the tarmac.

BORDER LINE

On the single track tramway between Bexley and Woolwich, one rail was in London and the other in Kent.

BARGAIN

Keighley Corporation paid only £5 for the two and a half miles of tram tracks it acquired from the Keighley Tramways Company in 1894.

TRACKED DOWN

For taking three tons of tramlines worth £10 from the tracks in Blackfriars Road, London, in 1953, three men were fined a total of £50.

DEAD END

A tramway in Yorkshire "started where nobody lived and finished where everybody was dead." It was opened in 1903 by Mid-Yorkshire Tramways Company between the Thackley-Windhill boundary near Bradford and Nab Wood Cemetery—a distance of about three miles.

Lucky for some

WINNING LINE

A "tramway tombola" was held at Falkirk, in Fife, during 1918 to help the war effort. For penny tickets sold by conductresses, prizes from £1 to £200 could be won in monthly draws. More than 125,000 tickets were sold some months.

Weekly lotteries were held on the number of the first tram to leave the Rhondda tram sheds each Sunday morning. The lotteries were illegal, however, and summonses resulted in one man and eleven boys appearing before Ystrad justices on one occasion.

WHERE THERE'S A WAY THERE'S A WILL

A Portuguese ship broker left 24 Liverpool tram drivers £1 each in his will in 1940 for the cheery words they exchanged with him during his 30 years of daily tram travel.

MUSICAL CONDUCTORS

A competition held in Berlin for the best tramway song written by a tram conductor attracted 60 entries. A book of the songs was published by Berlin's Association of Tramway Employees.

WHISTLE STOP

To stop horse tramcars on Eccles Old Road, Salford, a local alderman blew a whistle. He sat on the open top deck and gave his regular crew £5 at Christmas if they made sure his seat was kept clear of rainwater and snow.

TOKEN FIND

Beachcombing with a metal detector, a Sussex man found a mixed assortment of treasure, including coins, musket balls and, of all things, a New York tram token.

SMELLING AND SELLING LINE

Manure sold by the Liverpool United Tramways and Omnibus Company fetched between 2s 6d and 3s 6d a ton depending on which stable it came from. Manure sales earned the Company 0.01d for every car mile run.

The tram on the left won first prize in a competition for the best decorated tram at Burton-upon-Trent in 1908.

Manchester tram employees were keen musicians and formed bands at Queens Road and Hyde Road depots and this banjo, mandolin and guitar orchestra at Birchfields Road.

Ideal vehicle

"For short journeys in a city, the tram seems the ideal vehicle. It is easy to enter and leave, and it holds a great many people. One knows not merely where it is at any instant, but where it is not and never can be. It cannot, like a bus, pursue one all over the road. It is subject to the predestination of its rails, whereas the bus is a freelance, and can chase its victim everywhere except up trees."

—Hawick Express

"With so many trams either under restoration or operating these days, perhaps someone may suggest a television programme on do-it-yourself tramcar maintenance. If BBC 'Nationwide' can devote time to revealing such esoteric secrets as how to cure balding parrots, perhaps a ten-minute slot on how to change brake shoes does not seem too absurd."

—Rev. David Tudor of the National Tramway Museum

"The tram is the safest of all vehicles, and it can also usually be kept running in fogs. In fact, one of the most unexpected experiences for people in Doncaster after buses took over was the suspension of all services in thick fog."

—Doncaster Corporation Transport

"There are many people who have caught the irritating habit of talking about 'fixed' tracks or rails in connection with tramways—as if there were any other sort."

—Modern Tramway

"Apparently modern trams are silent, swift and comfortable. The old groan of the brakes, so painful and complaining, has been replaced by nothing more than a little hiss. A tram is obviously not a tram any more."

—Manchester Guardian

"Was not amused at being likened to a donkey . . ."

Childish pranks

A Manchester tram driver scratched his head in bewilderment as he drove through Gorton one Shrove Tuesday. Pedestrians on the pavements were laughing at him for no apparent reason.

It wasn't until he was driving down Hyde Road that he discovered the reason for their merriment—a carrot swinging to and fro just above his head.

The carrot was dangling on the end of some string suspended from the upstairs balcony by four students. The driver, not amused at being likened to a donkey, fetched a policeman to order the students off.

Students found trams a wonderful vehicle for their pranks and constantly caused crews anguish, despair and frustration.

They raced up and down gangways, flung satchels and caps at each other, shot peas and flicked tickets, swung on ceiling straps, opened windows, pulled trolley booms off the wires, smeared blacking on hand rails, threw stink

"When the string became entangled in the moving cable, it pulled the rattling cans down the streets . . ."

bombs and hid rotting fish heads in destination boxes and under seats.

They also chalked slogans and banalities on dashes and rocker panels, like "It's quicker to walk," "Reserved for firewood," and "Knickers."

Inside the cars they carved their initials on the wooden panelling and seat rests. Did George's love for Doris ever lead to marriage? Where today is Rosie—that indefatigable scratcher whose name appeared on nearly every Stalybridge tram?

Many parents today recall the thrill they got from running up and down the top deck gangway and knocking back seat rests so that they made a nerve-racking clatter, like a round of machine-gun fire.

And there was a wonderful feeling of devilment in turning the handles of destination boxes so that the blind read "Depot Only." These were temptations too great to resist.

When leaving trams, one of the most popular pranks, always conducted with the greatest relish, was to jump heavily on the sand pedal on the platform, so that at least a bucketful of sand was deposited on the rails.

Another delight was to swing round the brass platform rails, like a monkey on a stick—a dangerous practice, but exhilerating.

There was also the fun of putting coins and other objects on the tram tracks and seeing them flattened under the wheels of passing trams.

Ordinary pins, for instance, could be turned into scimitars or swords for toy soldiers. And in Liverpool it was the favourite means of turning a metal trouser button into a "delly," which was the alley in the scouse variant of marbles.

A favourite pastime of children in Edinburgh, in the days of the cable cars, was to tie string to a tin can and drop the string down the cable slots between the tracks. When the string became entangled in the moving cables it pulled the rattling cans down the streets.

In 1902 ten boys were taken to court for this prank. Their punishment, fortunately for them, was a gentle admonishment from the judge, who had great difficulty in keeping his face straight. The practice didn't please the Edinburgh tramways management, for the cans fouled up the cable winding gear in the power houses.

Boys who were the most unpopular with managements, however, were those who carried screwdrivers and surreptitiously tried to sabotage trams by undoing round-headed screws that held vital parts together.

One boy confessed later in life that he had tried to remove at least half a dozen screws every time he took a ride in the hope of seeing at least one car fall apart before his schooldays were over.

In London, too, students were just as devilish. On occasions you would see a growing line of trams outside St. Thomas's Hospital because their wheels were unable to get a grip on the track. The reason? Medical students had soaped the rails.

There are a number of cases of children trespassing in tram depots, driving trams up and down and crashing them. Mischievous boys caused some damage at the Grimsby and Cleethorpes sheds in 1925.

They entered the depot unobserved and boarded a car standing on one of the tracks.

One of them found a controller key and started the car, which ran forward and bumped into another car, causing a third tram to crash into the wall of the depot. The impact broke some windows and did other damage.

The boys ran away, leaving the current switched on. This caused a resistance coil to become overheated, and insulation melted and caught fire. The flames, however, were quickly extinguished by depot staff who arrived on the scene.

Another prank particularly aggravating for tramway crews was for boys to jump on the cars and ring the emergency stopping signal. It sometimes resulted in passengers being shaken or hurt when drivers applied the brake fiercely.

Two Croydon boys who were caught redhanded performing this prank in 1917 were each fined five shillings.

By contrast there were many children who were anxious to help tramway workers, rather than hinder them. To help conductors they dutifully turned seats over at terminuses and wound blinds to the correct destinations.

Some 50 Manchester Grammar School pupils helped Salford crews in the first world war by acting as trolley boys. The lads, who worked Friday evenings, Saturdays and Sundays, turned the trolley booms round and rang the bells for conductors.

At Birmingham, also in the first world war, boy scouts assisted women conductors on the Edmund Street routes during rush hours by ringing the bell and calling out the names of stopping places. When the conductresses had collected in all the fares, the scouts left the cars and returned to the Edmund Street terminus to board other full cars.

Assisting with the trolley boom was not as easy as it looked—as a Reading boy found out when one of his good deeds turned sour and brought a large part of Reading's trams to a halt.

He had seen conductors race up the stairs to haul in trolley booms that dewired. So when the boom swung loose one morning he leapt into action, seized the trolley rope and pulled on it.

"Unfortunately, I wasn't quick enough, or perhaps strong enough, and the boom jammed in a bracket that held up the overhead wire," he said. "The wire snapped and a length of it fell into the road in a shower of sparks, narrowly missing a very startled cyclist."

The exploit earned him the gratitude of his schoolfellows, however, since they all had to walk to school and were very late.

Trams carried millions of children to and from school, and many parents and grandparents today have fond memories of school journeys they made

Young visitors to the National Tramway Museum at Crich, who have never savoured the joys of riding to school on a tram, are shown how the controls of a Blackpool and Fleetwood toastrack-type car are operated.

by tram. Like Mrs. Lorraine Gough of Kirkhouse Street, Pontypridd, who was given a halfpenny by her mother to ride home on the tram if the weather was bad.

Said Mrs. Gough: "It always infuriated my mother that when rain or snow forced me to use the tram I arrived home drenched.

"That was because we always travelled on the open top deck. None of us kids could see the logic of not having the adventure of climbing those rocking twisting stairs and fighting for the front seat so that we could watch the driver and laugh at the water dripping down his collar, helped on its way by our vicious little hands, be it ever on my conscience."

She also recalls that if she had had a row with her school-mates, she turned over the back rest of the seat so that she could sit back to back with her enemies. "We were then able to use 'banging heads' tactics," she explained.

"Nevertheless, we were never destructive, and the tram crews behaved like devoted fathers, and we really did respect them. No journeys that I have taken since have been so memorable as those halfpenny windy wet rides on those gorgeous open-top trams, with the fascination of watching the driver change from one end to the other for the return journey, carrying his OXO box and bottle of cold tea."

Many tramcars were hired to carry children on social outings—to parks, zoos, museums, fetes, picnics, carnivals, royal visits and other events.

The biggest number of children to be carried by tram to one event was probably in Sydney, Australia, in 1954, when 70,000 children were mass lifted to the Showground for the Royal Tour.

In Manchester, 100 special trams took children into the city centre for the opening of the Central Library by King George and Queen Mary in 1934. All the destination blinds were set at "Special", except on one car, where the boys on board had altered them to read "All Saints"—the name of one of Manchester's busiest tramway junctions. The joke was not lost on people waiting at stops for ordinary service cars.

Children could see the humour in destinations shown on the front of trams—like Spital Tongues in Newcastle, Foggy Furze in West Hartlepools, Tooting and Barking in London, Idle in Bradford, Loose in Maidstone, Sandal in Wakefield and Borstal on the Chatham system.

Tickets, too, were an endless source of fascination. They served as toothpicks, whistles, hatband decorations, darts, rings, aeroplanes, concertinas, chains, window wipers, book marks, visiting cards, catapult ammunition, peashooters, and, in fact, a thousand and one things, for childhood imagination knew no bounds.

In Glasgow, children believed that if they collected enough tickets with the number seven anywhere in the serial number they could get a limbless ex-serviceman a wooden leg.

Flight Lieutenant G. R. Sunderland of Bugbrooke in Northamptonshire recalls the fun Bradford schoolchildren had with tickets. They used to stick them in the bowler hats of office workers.

"When the tram reached the city centre the office workers queued down the stairs in readiness for their stop," he said. "While they waited they had the ribbon of their bowlers festooned with tickets, stuck in by schoolboys occupying the balcony seat at the head of the stairs."

Some children were so fascinated by tickets they even resorted to stealing them.

At Nottingham Children's Court in 1917 it was stated that it was a common practice for boys to jump on the trams as they were moving, steal a quantity of tickets while the conductor was busy collecting fares on the upper deck, and jump off again.

Two lads caught redhanded were each ordered to pay 2s 6d costs for stealing 400 tickets.

Today, it would not be surprising if a child did not know what a tram was. But a survey conducted at an infant school in Stockport produced some surprising results.

Nearly a third of the children questioned said it was a "kind of bus running on track with wires," 19 replied a "kind of train," seven said it was a "bus," two a "kind of bus and train," three a "car," three a "coach" and two "something with an engine in it." Nine were quite clear in their minds that a tram ran on lines, and to avoid any confusion two of them did a drawing of one.

"A tram rides on four wheels; it goes up and down hills, and it takes people in it," said one child.

"A tram goes on lines; it carries people to over blases," explained another.

One of the most descriptive answers was: "A trame is a big cind of train and it gows on the train line and it gows slow and sum tims it gow verye fast and it works by electicitice and it is litid up and it looks verye nise."

Three children said a tram was an "old man," one said it was a "kind of fish" and another thought it was a "flag."

There were only 18 who did not know what a tram was.

Pearly queen

I remember, I remember
A tram ablaze with light,
All double-decked with fairy-lamps
Upon a gala night.
It glided into Battersea
To Bow and Bethnal Green,
A blowsey, frowsy London tram—
To me, a pearly queen.

—Anon

Specials

CAMEL POWER

Camels hauled the Tehran trams, some of which were reserved specially for Moslem women.

TRAM SLEEPERS

Sleeping cars were provided on some long-distance tramways in America. The first ran between Columbus and Cincinnati (Ohio) in July 1903.

FIRST-CLASS

First-class trams were used in Liverpool between 1908 and 1923. They were painted in distinctive cream and the seats upholstered in blue.

EXPRESSLY FOR OVERTAKING

Express trams ran on Dublin's Dalkey services between 1908 and 1914. They overtook other trams at special loops laid at Ballsbridge and Booterstown.

GUARDED

Armed naval guards travelled on the trams running between Piraeus and Perama in Greece. The trams served a jetty used by boats from the Royal Hellenic Navy's dockyard.

ONE CAR A DAY

Regular tramway services operated by the Nottinghamshire and Derbyshire Tramways Company ceased on 30 December, 1932, but one car a day was run for legal reasons until 4 October, 1933.

LAST BUT NOT LEAST

Packed like sardines, 136 passengers crammed on Warrington's last tramcar on 28 May, 1935. The tramcar (No. 1) normally seated 58. Built in 1902, it ran 777,600 miles during its 33 years' service, carrying 9,652,000 passengers. The town's oldest surviving motorman drove it on its last trip, with his son conducting.

Nursery rattler! Babies in Bury had their own special tram before the first world war—to take them to a town-centre nursery each morning at six.

Stranded in the snow. A Bolton tram stuck in drifts on the Westhoughton route after more than 20 inches of snow had fallen in January, 1940. It was more than a week before the car was freed.

Indicators

SEEING HOW THE WIND BLOWS

Wind gauges or anemometers were used on hilly tram routes at Halifax, Cheltenham and Llandudno. When winds reached gale force, the trams were halted. The gauge at Halifax was put up at Crow Point on the route to Queensbury after two tramcars were blown over in a gale at Catherine Slack, more than 1,050 feet above sea level.

ALL CLEAR

A siren was fitted to a South Shields tramcar in place of the usual gong. According to one newspaper correspondent, it caused "old ladies to jump and scream, while youngsters ran whitefaced into shop doorways for safety."

FOG FLAGS

Coloured flags were flown on the trolley ropes of Merseyside trams when it was foggy to indicate whether the ferries were running. A square blue flag on a Wallasey tram meant no ferry from New Brighton and a red pennant no ferry from Egremont.

TWIN BOOMS

To protect the delicate instruments at Greenwich Observatory in South London, the tramway between Woolwich and Eltham was fitted with twin overhead wires and the trams with twin trolley booms, like trolleybuses. The second wire was used for return current, the usual earthed return not being allowed.

IN BLACK AND WHITE

On Chatham's trams, destinations were shown twice at both ends—in white on black and black on white.

FULL STOP

The tram stop sign outside the Swan and Sugarloaf public house in Croydon was fixed to a post which also carried the sign for the public house, a street lamp, a car park sign and a public lavatory sign. The post was hollow and served, in addition, as a vent for a drain.

Trams, like jet aircraft today, have been subject to hijacking and hold-ups, especially in Ireland during the troubles. In Dublin, trams were also overturned and used as barricades, and destination boxes were occasionally used as hiding places for revolvers.

Dreadful deeds

A conductor was forced to drive a hijacked London tramcar with a pistol pointed at his head.

It happened on the morning of 23 January, 1909, when two Russian anarchists attempted to make a get-away by tramcar after committing an armed robbery. The men were Jacob Lepidus and Paul Hefeldt from the Baltic port of Riga, who had come to Britain to raise money for Russian revolutionists and to enlist the help of exiles.

Their mission did not go as planned and so they resorted to armed robbery, snatching £80 from the pay clerk of a Tottenham rubber works. The clerk had just been to the bank to collect the cash and was getting out of one of the firm's cars when he was attacked.

The alarm was immediately raised, and men from the factory and the nearby police station were soon pursuing the robbers, who were armed with revolvers of the "newest and most deadly type" and many rounds of ammunition.

By the time the two men had reached the Walthamstow Corporation tramway on the main road to Chingford, they had killed a policeman who tried to stop them, injured several of their pursuers, and shot dead a 10-year-old boy who had accidentally run into their line of fire.

They had reached the tramway by fleeing down side streets and crossing the Lea marshes and the grounds of Salisbury Hall.

By now, 100 policemen were involved in the chase, some on horseback and bicycles, some in cars and some on foot. Many of them had been issued with arms. Roadblocks were being set up all over the area.

Meanwhile, Walthamstow tramcar No. 9, manned by driver Joseph Slow and conductor Charles Wyatt, was rolling peacefully towards the town centre. It was hailed by Hefeldt and Lepidus, and the driver, oblivious of the dramatic circumstances, quickly applied his brakes.

When the Russians leapt on board, brandishing a revolver, Slow fled upstairs in terror, and it was then that Wyatt was forced to take over the controls.

Wyatt had never driven a tramcar before, but realising how desperate the two anarchists were, he quickly set the car in motion.

"When I saw my driver make for the top deck and felt the revolver muzzle at my cheek, I thought the end had come," he said.

While the conductor drove the tram at full speed down the road, Lepidus continued to fire at the pursuing police from the back platform. Several shots fired by the police smashed the windows of the tram and splintered the interior woodwork. Miraculously, a woman and child in the lower saloon escaped injury.

An old man, the only other passenger on the car, attempted to disarm Lepidus, but was shot in the neck.

Upstairs, the driver was crouching down low to escape the hail of bullets fired by the police. He said: "When the tram started moving I peered over the front and saw that Wyatt was being made to drive. I kept hidden."

Wyatt prayed that Slow wouldn't do anything that endangered himself and the passengers. He said: "I was frightened he might halt the car by cutting the circuit. If he had done that the ruffians might have shot me dead, thinking I had stopped the car."

Meanwhile, the police had commandeered a tramcar going in the opposite direction and had ordered the driver to give chase.

After driving for a mile, Wyatt pointed out to Hefeldt that there was a police station ahead. At first, Hefeldt didn't believe him, but when he realised the conductor was speaking the truth, both hijackers jumped off the tram and made off on board a milk van, after shooting the milkman in the chest and arm.

Crashing the van a short distance later, they hijacked a horse and cart, but by then the net was tightening. Cornered against a high fence, Lepidus turned his gun on himself, and Hefeldt was shot dead by the police when trapped in the bedroom of a house.

Three policemen and 14 others were injured during the chase, in addition to the two who were killed. Strangely enough, the £80 stolen by the two Russians was never recovered.

There are cases of other tramcars being held up by armed criminals.

Only a year before the London incident, two Cairo trams were attacked by a band of ruffians armed with bludgeons. The assailants stopped the cars, which were packed with passengers returning from a popular afternoon resort, and struck the conductors. They then wounded and robbed a number of the passengers, depriving women of their jewels and ornaments and the men of their watches and purses.

In America, another gang of desperados held up a tramcar near San Francisco in 1912, emptying the pockets of all 80 passengers on board and grabbing the crew's takings.

The police in pursuit by tram . . . a scene of yesteryear re-enacted at Detroit, where an old-style tramway has been built as a tourist attraction. Opened in 1976, the line runs down Washington Boulevard and is operated with restored cars, like this rebuilt 1900 Lisbon model.

Even horse tram passengers had to suffer the indignity of being held up by bandits. Some late-night travellers on a horse tramcar in Melbourne were robbed of their belongings by a masked gang of four in 1901.

The car was the last one of the night to Auburn and was hailed by two men shortly after midnight. The driver thought they were prospective passengers and started to pull up. He realised his mistake too late when one of the robbers swung aboard wielding a revolver.

"Do as you're told or I'll spill your brains on the floor," ordered the robber as he pressed the revolver against the driver's cheek.

Two more of the gang jumped on the rear platform, pushed the conductor into the saloon, and ordered the passengers to empty their pockets, while the fourth bandit kept watch outside the car.

The gang got away with more than £100.

But robbers didn't always get their own way. Two thugs who tried to hold up a streetcar at Lima (Ohio) in 1900 fled in fear when the driver produced a revolver and started firing at them. While at Bridgeton in New

Jersey four bandits were lucky to escape with their lives when they were set upon by passengers and thrown into the road.

In New York in 1908, a middle-aged woman suffered a horrible death by being pushed under a tramcar. Two men had attempted to rob her, but she struggled and ran away. The men chased her and pushed her across the tracks in front of a tramcar that was passing. The tram crew saw the attack, but were unable to stop the car in time. It ran over the woman and killed her.

Even more horrifying was a murder in Vincennes in 1904. A waiter was knocked down by a tram while crossing the street. Although drawn into the car's truck mechanism, he was not hurt and called upon the driver to send for assistance to raise the car to set him free. The driver, however, declared that if the man did not get out at once he would start the car. As the waiter did not move, the current was switched on, and the car passed over his body, almost severing it in two.

In Ireland in 1920, an elderly magistrate was dragged off a Dublin tramcar and shot dead on the roadside. He was Alan Bell, who had the unenviable job of tracking down Sinn Fein bank deposits and impounding them.

The assassination took place in broad daylight. Mr. Bell was travelling on a tramcar bound for Kingstown, when six armed men climbed aboard, tapped him on the shoulder and told him: "Come on Mr. Bell, your time has come."

Two tramway officials who thought "their time had come" were Birmingham tramways superintendent Leonard Johnson and Derby tramways manager Frank Harding.

Leonard Johnson was shot by John Henry Cuttler, a 60-year-old traffic inspector, at the Birmingham tramways headquarters in 1925. It happened after a row between the two men over staffing levels at the Tennant Street premises.

Johnson had refused to let Cuttler have more men, and during the argument Cuttler pulled out a revolver. There was a scuffle and shots were fired, one of which wounded Johnson.

Office clerks, hearing the rumpus, dashed into the office and overpowered Cuttler, who later admitted to the police that he had fired the revolver.

Cuttler, charged with attempted murder, maintained that he had not intended to fire the revolver. He said that Johnson jumped at him and that the revolver went off accidentally in the ensuing struggle.

The man defending him was the famous barrister Norman Birkett, then virtually unknown, who pointed out that Cuttler had been a crack shot during the several years he had spent in Africa.

"Can you believe that Cuttler deliberately fired? At six feet he failed to kill. He almost failed to wound, and yet he is a champion revolver shot!" said Mr. Birkett.

After retiring for more than an hour, the jury found the traffic inspector "not guilty."

The Derby tramways manager, Frank Harding, was threatened with a revolver by a former conductor in 1907.

The conductor, who had been sacked three months before, went to the tramway offices and told the caretaker that he had come to blow out the brains of the manager. He held the manager responsible for the circumstances which led to his dismissal.

In his defence it was said he had got into bad company and had had too much to drink, and that the threats were simply swagger. He was sent to prison for two months, with hard labour.

Tramway crews, more than officials, have also suffered from attacks by passengers, and typical of these was an assault on a Bolton driver and conductor in 1906.

The conductor had rung the tram away from a stop on the Great Lever route, when a young man and his father came down from the top deck and asked him to stop. The conductor said they would have to wait until the next stopping place. The young man then tried to ring the bell, and when the conductor stopped him, he seized the conductor by the throat and attempted to throw him off the car.

Passengers alerted the driver, who stopped the car and dashed to the rescue of his mate. The young man released his hold of the conductor, and instead grabbed the driver by the throat, only leaving hold when a policeman arrived. By then the driver was black in the face.

In court, the young man maintained that the conductor had laughed when he asked him to stop the car, and that the driver had used threatening behaviour. Found guilty of both assaults, he was bound over for a month and fined.

Many assaults on crews took place at night—particularly after licensing hours, when drunkards boarded the trams.

At Doncaster, however, there was one tram on which the driver and conductor felt very secure, and this was the car that carried the police to the racecourse on St. Leger Day.

Tramcars which were not too popular with crews, on the other hand, were those used to convey criminals at Bristol, Montreal and Sydney.

At Bristol, prisoners were taken by tram between Horfield Prison and Lawford's Gate Police Court, but the practice ceased in 1911 after complaints from other passengers.

Montreal had two tramcars, sheathed in steel and painted black, which carried prisoners between the Champ de Mars courthouse and the city's Bordeaux Prison.

Sydney also had a tramcar, No. 948, which was specially built in 1909 to convey prisoners. The black Maria of the tramways, it was a formidable and forbidding vehicle, and nobody had ever escaped from it—until 4 March, 1946.

On that day, the tram was lumbering with grim purpose down the street when suddenly two men appeared on the roof, jumped off with cat-like agility and scampered towards Centennial Park as fast as they could.

They were 25-year-old housebreaker Darcy Ezekial Dugan and 18-year-old Robert Porter Lewis, and they were being taken by the tram from Long Bay gaol to Darlington Court in the same way countless thousands of other prisoners had been carried before. But Dugan had a reputation as the Houdini of the New South Wales penal system—and escaping from Sydney's prison tram was no less difficult for him than escaping from the police van that had attempted to take him to court only a fortnight before.

The police thought he would be secure in the prison tram, which had carried seven condemned men to the Long Bay gallows.

It had six strongly-barred cells, with 50mm thick walls and steel floors. They locked him in the tram for the trip to court with a number of other prisoners.

But Dugan had somehow laid hold of a knife and while the tram was moving he cut a hole in the roof, which was made of thinner metal.

Dugan and Lewis were captured during the evening of the next day after a manhunt involving 300 policemen. Nobody else ever escaped from the tram, which is now preserved in the Sydney tramway museum at Loftus in New South Wales.

By request

Diving down the Kingsway Tunnel like the gaping jaws of hell
To the river where you'd give her all you'd got.
Oh, the sight of sparks a-flying!
Oh, the jangling of the bell!
Oh, the scent of wooden brake-blocks running hot!

From Woolwich Park to Camberwell
From Highgate Hill to Bow
On to Wapping
Only stopping by request!
Down a hill or round a bend
We would drive at either end.
And we never knew which end we loved the best!

—Anon

Objects of beauty

"For seventeen years members of this Society have laboured to create the tramway system you see today. It is the work of their own hands, in their own time at their own expense. Many trams have been transformed from virtual heaps of junk to objects of beauty. This has involved reviving forgotten crafts and encouraging young men (and sometimes women) to rediscover a standard of workmanship which many of us thought had disappeared."

—Major Charles Walker, Vice-President, National Tramway Museum

"New responsibilities will be added to royalty if hard-worked kings and princes, in addition to laying foundation stones and planting trees, are to be called upon to drive tramcars."

—The Tatler

"Others will sentimentalise—and argue—about the old coloured trams, the halfpenny fares, the miracles wrought by the late Mr. Dalrymple, the advent of the 'Green Goddesses,' and the legend of the trams that disappeared down a hole in Argyle Street and the policeman who, when informed of this mishap, asked 'Wass it a big hole?' "

—Glasgow Herald

"I have the impression that if a Liverpool bus, or even a Liverpool tram, trundled through one of these Belgian or Dutch cities, the local inhabitants would turn out in fun to cheer. Or jeer. Put one of the Belgian or Dutch streamliner trams on the tracks in Liverpool and it would create a sensation."

—Liverpool Express reporter

"Live metal pads, six inches or so square, were spaced at about three-yard intervals down the track, and some low-slung protuberance in the tram's hard underbelly stroked these in passing. It was locomotion by means of the kiss of life. The Wolverhampton tram tick-tocked its way to Penn Fields or Bushbury like Captain Hook's crocodile."

—BBC Home Service

Majestic

KING-SIZE TIP

The King of Rumania sometimes travelled with his subjects on the trams. The conductor of a car was much embarrassed when he recognised the King on one occasion in 1914 as he did not know whether he should ask for a fare or not. The King paid his fare, but not the ordinary one. He handed the equivalent of eight shillings, and insisted that his change should not be returned to him, leaving the conductor wishing he had royal passengers every day.

King Albert of the Belgians also liked travelling on tramcars. One day in 1924 the royal motorcar in which the King was travelling was held up by a slippery road surface. King Albert jumped out of his limousine, hailed the first passing tram, paid his fare, and alighted at the palace gates.

NAMED AFTER ROYALTY

Blackpool's open-top car No. 706 was named "Princess Alice" by the Princess herself when she visited the resort in 1985. She was presented with a book and Wedgewood plate issued to celebrate the centenary of Blackpool's trams.

DUCHESS SPECIALS

The Duchess of Northumberland hired six London United tramcars to take guests to a garden party at her home in Isleworth. All the seats were covered with white cloth and the stairs with a special woollen fabric.

HAIL CAESAR

The names of Roman emperors, such as Vespasian, Julian and Hadrian, were given to South Shields tramcars.

At Darlington, two horse cars were called Nelson and Wellington.

BOGEY CAR

Scratched into the woodwork on one of the Powell-Hyde cable cars in San Francisco are the words: "H. Bogart rode on this car circa 1946-7."

"Hailed the first passing tram . . ."

To the point

DEGREES OF CONDUCT

A conduct register was kept by the Falkirk tramways before the first world war and there was a points scale for bad behaviour. Failing to set destination screens properly or punching tickets incorrectly was 10 points, while running a car off the rails was 50 points. Smoking on duty was punished by three days suspension. Calling at a public house while on duty resulted in dismissal.

CONDUCTORS' DEGREES

Young men with degrees issue tickets on Italian trams. Many graduates are unable to obtain jobs suitable to their qualifications and instead they become tram drivers and conductors.

MISSED HER OWN TRAM

A Manchester tram conductress was fined in 1942 for being late 51 times during a period of 336 days, and for being absent without excuse on 43 days.

One day in the same year, between 350 and 400 Manchester tram workers were absent through sickness and other causes. Their duties had to be carried out by 100 members of the office staff.

JUDICIOUS IDEA

Judges in Saarbrucken were given courses in tram-driving in 1964—to help them judge traffic cases involving trams.

LONG WAIT

There were 10,000 names on the waiting list for people applying to become tram conductors at Liverpool in 1926.

WORKING HOLIDAY

A Croydon councillor spent his Easter holiday driving trams in 1917. He had learnt how to drive during a strike the previous year.

OVER THE TOP

For allowing passengers to ride on the roofs of its cars, Dudley and Stourbridge Electric Traction Company was fined 20 shillings.

A tight squeeze. Head-room on both decks of Cardiff's trams was much lower than average because cars had to pass under low bridges on all but two of the city's routes. Extensive trial runs were made before the final height of the cars could be determined.

Women took over tram driving duties from men in both world wars. Here, Mrs. Louie Lyons drives a tram through Manchester's Piccadilly in April, 1944.

Battling through

A Coventry boy was lucky he wasn't in bed on the night of 14 November, 1940. For that was the night a length of tram track weighing several hundredweight landed on his bed.

It was hurled there in a ruthless German air raid which wantonly destroyed much of Coventry and blasted the city's tramway out of existence.

Bombers flew over the city from nightfall to dawn, dropping hundreds of tons of bombs and reducing the city centre to a pile of rubble.

Craters were left all along the lines, making them completely impassable and some setts and pieces of track were found a quarter of a mile from the nearest tram routes.

A member of the transport department reported: "A complete tramway crossing was blasted over a three-storey house onto a back lawn, and it took five men to move it away."

All the wires were down in the city and Foleshill depot was isolated by craters on either side. In places lengths of rail were sticking 20 feet in the air.

Trams marooned by craters had to be derailed and hauled up side streets to get them back to the depot.

Ken Farrell, an authority on the city's tramways now living in the south, said: "I don't think anybody in Coventry that night will ever forget the raid. It was a nightmare and it took the city a long time to recover.

"The damage to the track was so great that the trams never ran again."

All the tracks were later dug up to help the war effort. They weighed 2,725 tons, which was enough metal to make 180 heavy tanks.

Bristol's trams, too, succumbed to bombing by Goering's Luftwaffe.

A high explosive bomb wiped out a depot full of trams at Bedminster on 4 January, 1941, and killed a driver who was about to take out an early workmen's car. It brought to an end services on the Bedminster Down and Ashton Gate routes.

In the same raid, another bomb hurled a tram into a butcher's shop. A pedestrian sheltering a few blocks away said: "I thought my number was up. There was a bright flash and the tram was lifted bodily off the track as if it was a lump of matchwood.''

The entire system was abandoned after another blitz four months later, on 11 April, when a bomb plunged through St. Philip's bridge, disconnecting the nearby tramway power station from the remaining routes.

A tram was ''frozen to the tracks'' during the earlier January raids, when temperatures were below freezing.

A direct hit had burst open a large water main, causing water to engulf a tram which earlier had been abandoned when the sirens sounded.

The water quickly turned to ice, leaving the tram frozen to its tracks.

A Bristolian who saw the stranded vehicle at the height of the raid could hardly believe his eyes.

Other tramways also badly damaged by bombing, like those in London, Birmingham and Sheffield, continued running despite many difficulties.

Employees worked hard and fearlessly to restore services, in some cases repairing tracks and clearing them of debris while bombs were still falling.

Three Birmingham employees who carried out rescue work in a blazing depot in 1942 were each awarded the B.E.M. They had dowsed themselves with buckets of water so that they could work in the intense heat.

The magazine *Modern Tramway* reported: ''Getting the trams running called in all cases for superhuman efforts on the part of the staff.

''In one town in the Midlands (Sheffield), a heavy bomb fell on the tracks and actually blew a tramcar in two, the top deck being blown some distance from the lower deck. A huge crater was made, yet a normal tram service was in operation within 48 hours.''

In many towns, tracks were built over craters, enabling services to carry on while repairs were still being made to mains and sewers, other traffic meanwhile having to be diverted.

''At one place where it was not possible to bridge a crater, permanent way staff showed great ingenuity by laying a temporary track round it,'' said *Modern Tramway.*

A London driver claimed there was a big advantage in driving a tram in the blitz. ''You can't hear a bomb coming or an aeroplane overhead. You don't know anything about what's happening. All you can hear is the tram going along,'' he said.

The havoc wreaked on British tramways, however, was nowhere near as great as that inflicted on those in Europe.

Scores of tramway workers were killed in the epic battle for Stalingrad, many of them bombed and machine-gunned at their posts. All the city's tramway depots and substations were destroyed in the fighting, and burnt-out tramcars littered the streets, which were strewn with damaged tracks and overhead.

Yet within a few months of the German retreat, the Russians had re-opened a five-mile stretch of line connecting the city centre with the factory district.

War bonds were sold inside this Liverpool tram posing as a tank in the first world war.

A Soviet trade union official, commenting on this achievement, said: "Everyone who has visited the city and seen its ruins, its pavements and roads ploughed up by shells and bombs, will realise what it must have cost the Soviet people in gruelling self-sacrificing labour to set those streets ringing cheerily with the familiar clatter and sound of the bells."

During the second world war, trams ran with white paint on the fenders, white tape on platform handrails, and masked headlights. Tram windows were covered with adhesive netting to minimise the effect of flying glass should they shatter in air raids. And a number of measures were also taken to cut down or obscure the flashing and sparking from overhead wires.

To avoid losing a whole depot full of trams, some authorities parked their cars apart in suburban streets. In Birmingham, cars were parked safely out of the way of other traffic on the grassed central reservations, where they were hidden by trees.

Unfortunately, while strategic parking went some way towards safeguarding the cars from bombing, it didn't protect them against hooligans, almost as rife then as now, and in one night in Leeds 200 lamp bulbs were stolen from 70 cars stabled in the streets.

"Picked out a Zeppelin over Barnet . . ."

Berlin's trams, like Birmingham's, were parked in avenues where trees sheltered them from overhead view. If one caught fire, the blaze was immediately tackled by the tramway system's own fire brigade.

London lost some 70 trams through air raids, and many others were badly damaged.

In one heavy raid in Birmingham in 1941, the tramway system was hit in 46 places, the worst damage being at Miller Street depot, which suffered a direct hit. The blast burnt out 18 cars and wrote off six others.

With many of its cars damaged and 14 completely destroyed in the bombing, Sheffield found it necessary to obtain 24 second-hand cars from Newcastle and Bradford in 1941 and 1942 to strengthen its sorely depleted fleet and so maintain services.

Tramway systems also suffered from bombing in the first world war. A Sunderland tram was destroyed in a Zeppelin raid in 1916, when a bomb landed on the Wheat Sheaf depot. An inspector and some people sheltering in the tram were killed and many tramway employees injured.

The same year, a Zeppelin bombed an all-night tram at Streatham in London, killing the crew and an inspector.

In another 1916 raid, a Walsall tram was damaged by bomb blast as it was travelling through the town.

The Mayoress of Walsall and her sister were on board when the bomb fell on Bradford Place. They were sitting in front of the car and were badly injured by flying glass. The Mayoress staggered to a nearby shop, but died later from her injuries.

In 1917, Norwich tramways arranged for aircraft warning notices to be fitted to its cars. These read: "Hostile Aircraft Approaching—Take Cover." Crews in those days were obviously pretty well informed or had good eyesight.

Lincoln gave warning that an attack was imminent by cutting the power off for a few seconds. A citizen said: "This was the signal for the cars to return to the depot.

"If a driver was on an outward track, he reversed the trolley and drove back down the wrong side of the road. You would sometimes see two cars racing neck and neck to see who could get back first."

Two tramways were bombarded by the Germans from the sea. One of them, the Giant's Causeway line at Portrush in Northern Ireland, miraculously escaped damage when a submarine, engaging the coaster "Wheatear," shelled Portballintrae for two and a half hours in May, 1914.

The other tramway, at Hartlepools, wasn't so lucky when German armoured cruisers shelled the town later the same year. A member of the staff was injured and buildings, cars and equipment damaged.

The manager reported: "A shell struck the office roof and carried part of it away. The flagstaff on top of the depot was splintered and overhead wires brought down in three places.

"Windows of several cars in service were shattered and a controller on one car standing in the depot was struck by a piece of shell which came through the depot window."

To help the war effort, some tramway depots were used to produce munitions.

Glasgow tramways started producing scarce munitions components in 1915, and at Reading munitions were produced in the tramway repair shops. Four bays of the Reading sheds were also used as an instructional bombing range for airmen, and some of the trams had to be left out in the open at night.

The South Lancs tramways turned its workshops at Atherton over to the manufacture of shells. Tramway historian E. K. Stretch said that some 1,000 shells a week were produced, and nearly all the office and maintenance staff, from general manager downwards, spent part of their working time on this job.

In the second world war, some towns that had scrapped trams agreed to dig up abandoned tram tracks and poles. It was estimated that each mile of track yielded up to 350 tons of top grade steel. Several thousand tons of rail were ultimately lifted and turned into armaments.

A small number of tramway systems opened up new lines to serve strategic installations, such as docks and airfields, and in the second world war a number of towns such as Coventry, Bradford and Bolton, reopened abandoned tram routes to save valuable imported fuel.

Norwich dug up some disused track and laid it in double quick time to an airfield and armaments works on Mousehole Heath in 1917.

Gloucester extended its Hucclecote route the same year, using abandoned track from the city centre, to serve a new airfield being built at Brockworth, so that wagons pulled by an old tram could deliver, first, materials needed to construct the airfield, and later aircraft parts.

Also in 1917, the Admiralty gave Dunfermline and District Tramways a grant of £25,000 towards the construction of a new line to the Royal Dockyard at Rosyth, but the laying of the track was completed too late to be of much benefit to the navy in the war.

Liverpool opened up a new tramway down the East Lancs Road to carry war workers in 1943. The tramway department's resourcefulness in providing services to factories earned a commendation from Minister of Labour Ernest Bevin. He said: "I know of no other district where they have been more helpful."

To cater for the growing numbers of munitions workers, Erith in South London acquired a second-hand tram from Hull in 1916. It was shipped by sea-going barge down the east coast and up the Thames.

In both wars, certain trams were able to play a more active role in the conflicts. In 1944, for instance, an abandoned Aachen tram became a "streetcar named death." It was packed with explosives by American troops and sent careering down a hill into German lines with devastating effect. The soldiers numbered it V13 and wrote other appropriate inscriptions on it.

On active service! A Bradford tram shows its mettle by hauling a gun carriage from Lister Park to Frizinghall in August, 1914.

During the Mexican revolutions of 1914-18, Mexico City trams were commandeered by rival generals and used as troop carriers, armoured units and mobile gun platforms.

In 1916 the War Office commandeered London trams and used them as searchlight carriers in Barkingside, Chadwell Heath, Croydon, Hounslow, Hampton Court, Bexley, Barnet and Enfield.

"The searchlight was mounted on the open top deck, the lower saloon being used to accommodate the generator and to provide a mess room," reported one observer.

The dark green cars were driven by men of the Royal Engineers who had been drivers in peacetime on the Tynemouth and South Shields tramway systems.

During a heavy raid in October, 1916, one of the tramcar searchlights picked out a Zeppelin over Barnet. Attacked by the Royal Flying Corps, the Zeppelin burst into flame and fell to the ground at Potters Bar. All its crew were killed and they were buried in Potters Bar churchyard.

Bradford trams rendered useful service by moving guns and munitions. Fitted with a special towing device, the cars were able to haul gun carriages and ammunition wagons six miles across the city from a territorial army camp at Lister Park to Frizinghall in 1914.

Harold Brearley of Idle, Bradford, has first-hand knowledge of the move.

"I was in the scouts running messages for the territorials," he said. "When the trams got to the city boundary, horses took over and pulled the guns to Skipton."

In response to Kitchener's appeal for more men, trams were pasted over with posters urging volunteers to join the forces, and sent on tours of suburban routes. Recruiting officers sat on board ready to sign up new volunteers.

Leeds tram posters said: "Nah then, John Willie. Ger agate lad, join t'army."

To support the recruiting campaign, some cars were made to look like tanks and armoured cars.

In Halifax, a single-deck car was converted into a food kitchen in 1918. Equipped with electric ovens, steamers, hot plates, boiling plates and a 100-gallon water tank, it could serve a thousand hot meals out of hatches on either side.

Men and women from factories welcomed the service. They could get soup or potatoes or a dumpling for a penny, vegetable pie for fourpence, and rice or ginger pudding for one and a half pence.

In Hamburg, in the second world war, trams were used to remove soil excavated for air-raid shelters.

Portsmouth put aside six of its trams in the first world war for naval and military hospital patients. They were used to take the patients to free afternoon concerts at the South Parade Pier.

In Wigan, convalescent soldiers at the several military hospitals in the town were given free passes to travel on the trams. The soldiers crowded on the cars in such numbers that ordinary passengers, including miners and other shift workers, were left standing at stops.

Most tramways allowed members of the forces to ride free. Hull estimated that this amounted to 100,000 rides a week on their cars, which made a big difference to takings.

"Although there were some people who objected to soldiers getting free rides, people didn't seem to mind," recalled a pensioner. "I can remember an elderly gentleman getting up and offering his seat to a soldier, and saying it was an honour to have him on the car."

Modern Tramway reported that during the 1939-45 war Liverpool trams carried four million Allied troops and half a million evacuees through the city. As many as 20 trams were in use at one time carrying troops. The trams were also used to distribute food.

Thousands of tramway crews joined the armed forces. Nearly 4,000

Off the the battle fronts. Thousands of tram drivers and conductors were among those who volunteered for the forces in the first world war.

Glasgow drivers and conductors fought in the first world war, an eighth of them being killed on the battlefields.

A quarter of them joined up within 24 hours of their manager, James Dalrymple, appealing for volunteers to form a tramways battalion, which became the 15th Battalion of the Highland Light Infantry.

James Dalrymple went on to persuade 10,000 men in Glasgow to join the forces. His efforts raised a brigade of artillery, two infantry battalions and five companies of engineers.

Recruiting campaigns left some systems with fewer than half their men. At Reading three quarters of the pre-war staff had left by 1917 to join the forces.

Because of staff shortages, services had to be drastically curtailed and cars became very crowded, 500 passengers managing to cram on three Belfast cars on one occasion.

The places of many tramway men in both wars were taken by women. The number of women employed increased from 1,200 in 1914 to 18,800 in 1918.

The women did their work as efficiently as the men, and in Wrexham not one of them had an accident. A number of undertakings kept some women on for a while after the war.

James Dalrymple said in 1917 that "they were rapidly coming to the point when a majority of the tramway staff at Glasgow would be of the gentler sex and that he would not hesitate to have the whole service run by women."

He paid his women drivers the same as men—29 shillings a week.

In Nottingham, when it was agreed to train 20 women as conductresses, preference was given to the wives of men in the forces.

A Chesterfield woman driver, recalling her years on the trams, said: "I loved the work. It was tiring at times and often cold, but I didn't mind that.

"There was a wonderful fellowship on the trams, and I kept in touch with nearly all the girls for many years afterwards."

She recalled that one of her fellow women drivers received an award for averting an accident by knocking aside a learner and applying the brakes on a tram that was about to crash into another. The tramway committee commended the woman for "her conduct, presence of mind and nerve."

Lily Hebblethwaite of Clay Cross also drove Chesterfield trams in the war. She said: "The first tram of the day was at 4.40 a.m. and the journey was three miles and the fare three pence.

"The day the war was over I was so excited I ran my tram straight into the sheds, and all the other girls followed."

Some passengers tried to take advantage of the women crews, and in Manchester one of them offered a conductress a matchbox for his fare. It was a move he quickly came to regret when he felt the sharpness of her tongue.

One woman conducting on the London trams in 1940 had her tickets kicked out of her hands and they all blew into the road. As conductresses

These first world war women tram drivers at Wrexham never had a single accident despite the fact that on many occasions the cars were packed with more than 100 passengers. Sat with them on the front row are the manager, chief inspector and an inspectress.

had to pay for shortcomings out of their wages she worked for next to nothing that week.

Some tramway men objected strongly to women being taken on in the first world war and went on strike, which didn't go down well with the men in the trenches.

"We are having things very rough over here," wrote one soldier fighting in France. "And I have not been to sleep for nearly a week.

"The Germans keep shelling us night and day, and every shell that comes over we think our birthday has come.

"Now I see the tram men are on strike. They want to send them to the front."

On one Lancashire tramway, whenever a woman inspector boarded a car, the driver applied his brakes hard, sending her flying to the front end. Conductors refused to hand her their waybills to check.

At Bradford in 1915, the tramway union told the management that they objected to women being employed until it was absolutely necessary.

By contrast, some systems had difficulty in recruiting even women, and at Chatham two local curates were taken on as part-time drivers, while at Wemyss, in Fife, some miners found it no physical hardship to drive trams part-time during the day after a gruelling night's shift down the pits. Dundee tramways employed partially-disabled soldiers as conductors.

In many towns, however, tramway crews behaved very patriotically, and did a lot to help the war effort. In Aberdeen they sent parcels to their colleagues at the front.

One Aberdeen private wrote back on Christmas Day in 1914 saying: "I received my parcel from the employees of the Corporation tramways today, and I thank them very kindly as it is very useful to me.

"Our battalion is having a pretty hot time just now. We have lost a good many men, but we have to expect that. I have been very fortunate myself, thank God, although I had a very narrow shave last Friday night, when we made a charge, but none of our chaps were touched.

"The Grenadier Guards and the Gordons lost a lot of men that night; the Germans were about 30 to our one, so we had no chance at all. We shall

Workmen demolish the decorative base of a tramway overhead side pole at Bolton to provide much-needed scrap metal for armaments during the second world war.

require a large amount of men out here yet to assist us, as we are outnumbered.

"We are four days and four nights in the trenches at a spell, and we are knee-deep in mud and water all the time.

"This being Christmas, both sides ceased firing the whole day, and our chaps left their trenches and went over to the Germans and wished them a Merry Christmas.

"Our chaplain also went up to the firing line. One of the German majors gave him a cigar for a souvenir, and he gave the major a small prayer out of his cap in return.

"He also read the burial service for 17 Germans. The major told him that they were quite fed up and wanted to stop. We started fighting again at five o'clock.

"I wish it was all over, as the trenches are not quite the best, but we are sticking it with a right heart."

Glasgow tramways organised collections of tobacco pipes for men in the forces, and despatched 30,000 of them within a few months of the war starting in 1914.

In the second world war, tickets were sold on Manchester and Stockport trams in aid of Spitfire funds. A number of aircraft were bought with the money, and given names linked with the two towns.

From 1940, "honesty" boxes on Glasgow trams were used for donations to the Glasgow War Relief Fund. The scheme was welcomed by conductors, because the amount of conscience money previously collected in the boxes had been used as a yardstick of their fare collecting efficiency.

Sheffield tramways held collections on behalf of a number of war funds during the 1914-18 war, donations being placed in the used ticket boxes. As much as £600 a week was collected this way.

Dundee tramways raised money for the Red Cross in 1918 by running tombolas using tram ticket numbers. In one week, three quarters of a million tickets were sold, the prizes being War Bonds and Savings Certificates.

The end of both wars was marked by special celebrations, with trams playing a big part in carrying the huge crowds of revellers that flocked to town centres on Armistice Night and VE Day.

At Bristol one driver got so drunk on Armistice Night that his controls were taken over by a jubilant airman who had driven a tram only once before.

Other towns, like Ayr in Scotland, hurriedly put illuminated cars on the road, after frantic searches for dust-covered bulbs and cables which had been put aside during hostilities.

Special welcome-home dinners, parties and concerts were held to celebrate the return of men from the fronts. Typical of these was the dinner held by Lowestoft tramways for its war heroes on the night of 15 May, 1919, at the Royal Hotel.

The menu included "electric" clear soup, "trolley head" cutlets, roast "armature" vegetables at a "high tension," and "spanwire" caramel.

Memorials were erected to tram drivers and conductors who lost their lives on the battlefields.

Glasgow's memorial to the 500 tramway men who died in the first world war was unveiled by James Dalrymple on 9 April, 1933, the nearest Sunday to the anniversary of the capture of Ayette by the Tramways Battalion.

As the immediate post-war years went by, women tram drivers and conductresses who had admirably stepped in the breach were replaced by men back from the fronts.

In Huddersfield, conductresses with more than two years' war service on the trams were presented with a silver and enamel brooch.

Most of the women accepted dismissal with good grace, but in Bristol after the 1914-18 war it wasn't as smooth a transition as might have been expected.

The conductresses refused to leave the trams and returning men were lucky to get even a menial poorly-paid depot duty.

It led to demonstrations, with demobbed soldiers stopping trams, emptying them of passengers and smashing in their windows. With the public on their side, a delegation of former tramway employees was ultimately received by officials of the Bristol Tramways and Carriage Company on 28 April, 1920.

Following the meeting, the remaining conductresses were dismissed and the men taken back in their place.

The old steam car

'Twas not sweet of old, as our love we told
On the top of the old steam car,
When a wand'ring breeze made us cough and sneeze,
With a smell, like rotten eggs and tar!

But the lights were low, and the pace was slow,
And the corner seats were cosy,
And many a miss has received a kiss
On the top of the car
From Perry Barr
Or the tram that came from Moseley!

—Anon

Waltzing on air

"Glasgow, for all its engineering and commerce, is the world of the pub, the dance hall and the super cinema, neatly portrayed for tram students by the Standard car, the Cunarder and the Coronation. The likeness is inescapable: the Cunarder is a vision of aisles, soft lights and waltzing on air, the Coronation has smart usherettes, moquette seats and a familiar ritzy decor, and the most typical Glaswegian of them all is the immortal Standard car, fifty years old, all dark wood and brass fittings and blue pipe-smoke in the (upper) saloon, rolling home with a slightly inebriated four-wheel motion that belongs to Will Fyfe's Glasgow as surely do the late night crowds singing on the upper deck. Half a century hard at work, bruised, battered and patched, a lifetime's savings gone with no sign of a pension, defying every known theory of vehicle life; no wonder they are loth to go, they know that Glasgow would never be the same without them."

—John Price, tramway historian

"Mr. Wilson Gibb's job as transport manager for Douglas Corporation is rather more varied than might be the case elsewhere. It's not every transport department that can sell manure to the parks department; that employs its own blacksmith and apprentices to make 200 pairs of shoes each season; or that needs to buy in 110 tons of hay and 50 tons of rolled oats a year, let alone renting winter grazing. The cost of feed has gone up 400 per cent in the past couple of years; horses have their own fuel crisis."

—The Guardian

"Accident statistics of practically all cities and towns operating trams, in Britain, in the United States, on the Continent and elsewhere, show the tram to be indisputably the safest road transport vehicle. Trams cannot skid, no matter what the condition of the road surface. They are compelled by law to carry efficient lifeguard fenders, and have extremely powerful quick-acting brakes which operate on the rails as well as the wheels. Pedestrians, cyclists and motorists can easily see where the tram runs and can avoid it without difficulty."

—C. R. Bizeray, author of "Towards Ideal Transport"

Fated

TWICE OVER

In carbon copy accidents, an open-top tramcar on the South Staffordshire tramways overturned twice with fatal results. Both accidents occurred at the same spot on the sloping Dudley to Wednesbury line in January. Both times the tram had run away driverless from the Dudley terminus after the guard, assuming the driver was on board, had released the rear handbrake. In the first accident, on 16 January, 1916, 16 passengers were injured, two of them dying later. In the second accident, on 4 January, 1917, 30 passengers were injured and a learner conductress killed. Both guards were found guilty of carelessness.

SHOT BY TRAM

A woman pedestrian in Ashton-under-Lyne was shot by a passing tramcar in 1927. Someone had placed a live cartridge on the lines in Cavendish Street, and it was detonated when a tramcar ran over it, the bullet hitting the woman in the leg.

HEAD START

When the head of the trolley pole on a Croydon tramcar flew off in 1927, it went straight through the window of a passing electric train and was carried to Victoria Station in London. The tramcar had been about to pass under Selhurst railway bridge, when the trolley pole came off and was held for a while by a supporting wire. Suddenly released, the arm shot up with such force that the trolley head was projected through the train window.

STOPPED IN THEIR TRACKS

Three Southampton tramcars parked on a storage track during the second world war were deliberately set off driverless down a main road by a young boy. One of the runaways crashed into a service car, injuring a passenger. The other two were stopped by a lorry driver who gave chase and eventually manoeuvred his vehicle in front of them, easing them to a halt with little damage.

Trams and trains ran side by side on the Sunday's Wells route in Cork, Eire. The tram passing the Cork and Muskerry train was built in 1920 to replace the original Car No. 3 destroyed in the burning of the city during the Irish troubles.

Motorcars were often squashed between trams in early silent films (such as Keystone Cops classics), but this incident was for real. It happened in more recent years in San Francisco.

Fancy that

TAXI TRAM

A man who missed the last car home at Burton-upon-Trent knocked up the manager of the local tramway service and asked if he could hire a special car for two shillings. After bargaining for half a crown, the manager took a tramcar out of the sheds and drove the man home himself.

TENPENN'ORTH

Two women and 40 children packed into a Leeds tram in the '50s and rode round for three quarters of an hour. The total cost—tenpence for two adult tickets. Under the regulations every child under five could travel free if with a fare-paying adult. The rules were changed shortly afterwards to allow only one child to travel free with an adult.

LONG RUN

A streetcar ran from Boston to New York in 1912—a distance of 260 miles. It went via Worcester, Springfield, Hartford, New Haven (where it stopped for the night) Bridgeport, Stamford, Port Chester and Mount Vernon, using existing lines, except over the Darien river, where a special track had to be laid. Actual running time was 18 hours, and the car was fitted with a buffet so that meals could be taken on the way by the two drivers and two conductors on board.

CORONER'S COURT

The Bushmills tram shed on the Giant's Causeway line in Northern Ireland was used as a coroner's court following a lifeboat disaster in 1889. The bodies of three men drowned in the disaster were conveyed to the shed by special tram.

LITERARY CONNECTION

The first man to drive a tram in Lincoln was foreman engineer W. H. Snow—grandfather of the famous writer C. P. Snow.

A fold-away tram. This miniature tramway, which gives children rides at fetes and other events, is easily dismantled and packed away in an Austin Allegro. It was made by electrical engineer Richard Wall of Great Barr, Birmingham.

Bright feature

"The first car that came was not the one he wanted, and as it started noisily away from the stop, he was astonished to see a coil spring suddenly ejected from one of the bogies. The spring landed at his feet, and the tram went on its way, seemingly little the worse. Nobody else waiting took any notice, but Mr. Goldberg still has the spring to remind him of his first encounter with Manchester's trams."

—Ian Yearsley in "The Manchester Tram"

"At last the trams are here; round the corner comes the huge mass like a small town hall on wheels, and the quiet respectability of Cheltenham is challenged by the sharp 'ting-tang' of the gong and grinding of the wheels in the rail grooves, together with the curious 'singing' of the wires as the trolley runs along them—all of them new features to Sleepy Hollow."

—Gloucestershire Graphic

"The day could well come when the tramcar will have to be reinstated. And if that happens, it will be a singularly bright feature in our march through technical revolution."

—John Peyton, former Conservative Minister of Transport

"The cream-painted 81 tram bound for the World Fair is so packed it would make a British busman go on strike again."

—Daily Express

"For years the flea was king of the horse-drawn tram. He lurked in the dusty luxury of the seats, getting a free ride through life and feeding copiously off the fare-paying passengers. A penny ride on a horse-drawn tram was a passport to a journey of such itching discomfort that most people preferred to walk."

—Evening Chronicle, Newcastle

"Vanished into thin air . . ."

Phantoms of the track

It was a black murky night in 1926. So black that the light from the gas lamps was reduced to a mere flicker in the clinging mist.

An empty tramcar groaned its way from Dewsbury to Ossett—the only sign of activity to penetrate the stillness.

At Chickenley Heath it stopped to pick up two men. They bounded up the twisting stairs effortlessly. A short while later the conductor followed them to collect their fares. But a shock awaited him. For when he reached the top deck he found the two men had completely disappeared. There was no sign of them anywhere. The upper saloon was empty.

The conductor went back downstairs, assuming that the men had gone down the front staircase. But they were not on the lower deck either.

Becoming alarmed, he stopped the car by ringing the emergency bell, and made a search back along the track, in case the men had fallen off. But to no avail. They had vanished into thin air.

Talking about the incident some years later, a retired employee in Batley said: "The crew never reported the incident to the tramway company. They were convinced that the men were ghosts and that nobody would believe their story".

In fact, there may have been a logical explanation for the men's disappearance. They could have been pranksters, and may have hauled themselves on to the roof through the balcony, climbing down when the crews were not looking. It's the kind of trick schoolboys sometimes played in broad daylight.

Whether or not the men were ghosts, the incident is an illustration of how scepticism about the supernatural makes rational people keep sightings to themselves rather than suffer ridicule from publicity.

Yet there is no reason why tram ghosts should be less plausible than, say, ghosts in mediaeval mansions.

There were those who thought the arrival of the electric tram, ablaze with light, would send the headless lantern-carrying street-walking spectres scurrying to spookier spots. What they didn't foresee was that trams would bring their own phenomena.

"While he cut her throat . . ."

The sparks that fell from the first overhead tram wires, for instance, were immediately blamed on gremlins and other supernatural powers. It was said that it was a sign of wrath; an omen boding ill fortune. Let the sparks fall on you and the consequences would be too terrible to contemplate.

Phantom trams appeared, coming from nowhere and disappearing into the blackness more silently than superseding trolleybuses ever did.

A ghost tram is reported to have run regularly in the early hours at Frizinghall, Bradford. Checks with Bradford tramways department confirmed no service cars were running when the ghost tram was sighted.

"I don't know what happened to it when the tracks were pulled up and trolleybuses took over," said tramway historian Stanley King of Heaton Road, Bradford. "If it continued running afterwards, it didn't leave any grooves in the tarmac."

One of the most frightening tramway apparitions was seen in Ireland. It appeared one night at the turn of the century shortly after a man had been killed by a Dublin and Blessington steam tram.

A local man who had been out to a fair for the day was walking home in the dark when he was struck on the shoulder by a strange figure.

At first he thought it was somebody walking along the road and tried to start up a conversation. But when the figure didn't reply and kept bumping into him, he knew that it was no mortal being.

In a cold sweat he rushed to a friend's house and hammered loudly on the door. The horrified expression on his friend's face, when he opened the door, made him turn round and for the first time he set eyes on the figure, which was completely headless.

In terror, both men rushed into the house, slammed the door behind them and started praying for all they were worth.

Whereas this ghost was seen by only the two men, thousands flocked to see a sinister apparition at a Jarrow house in 1913. The apparition was of a man holding a woman by the hair while he cut her throat.

It appeared every night for a whole week and police had difficulty in controlling the crowds.

The *Jarrow Express* said: "It continued so long as the electric trams were running. As soon as they ceased it vanished. Ghosts have always been credited with making an appearance at midnight—not going away then."

The mystery was eventually solved when it was discovered that the apparition was caused by passing tramcar lights being reflected off a silver vase in the window of a house on the opposite side of the road. The vase was removed and the ghost was never seen again.

In recent years a ghost has been heard twice prowling around Leeds tram No. 180 in the main depot at the National Tramway Museum at Crich. The first time footsteps were heard going past the car, and the second time its bell started ringing.

Both times there was nobody in the vicinity of the car, which during its service in Leeds killed a person.

Not so easy to explain is the startling experience of John Robert Pickering Jones, former tram driver, who lived in Sharples Street, Stockport.

Mr. Jones was driving his tram along Carrington Road towards Stockport on a foggy night when for no apparent reason he suddenly applied his brakes opposite the Vernon Picture House.

He couldn't imagine why he stopped. But stop he did, and out of the fog came an old man with a stick walking straight up the track towards him, before disappearing again into the fog.

Mr. Jones said: "There was no bell signal. It must have been providence that made me stop."

It wasn't providence that caused the trams in South Shields to stop for an hour on 30 October, 1930. The electric power mysteriously failed—and no cause for the breakdown could be found—no human or natural cause, that is.

If it was something supernatural behind the stoppage, Corporation officials took pains not to admit it.

Yet there are surprising examples of tramway operators heeding superstition.

For instance, a number of operators left 13 out of their fleet numbers to save themselves misfortune. There were no cars with the number 13 at Exeter, Leamington, Peterborough or on the Plymouth, Stonehouse and Devonport system.

Plymouth Corporation also left 13 out of its route numbers, as did Leeds Corporation.

But on the Tynemouth and District tramway system they paid the price for ignoring such important matters. Their tram 13 twice ran out of control on the steep one-in-ten gradient on Borough Road—in 1906 and, 13 years later, in 1919.

Bowing to influences obviously out of their control, the Company's officials changed the car's number to 11 after the second accident—and it ran safely from then onwards.

There's no doubt, however, that 13 was an unlucky number for Dartford tramways. They had 13 tramcars—12 double-deckers and one single-decker—all of which perished in a blaze at the tram sheds in 1917.

It is believed that the fire was started by a cigarette end left behind on one of the cars by a bank-holiday reveller the day before.

The major traffic for the Dartford trams was munitions workers, and because of this there had been a military guard at the depot, but it had been withdrawn only a few weeks before.

Strangely enough, as well as 13 trams, the depot held 13 barrels of oil, which were rolled away during the blaze. Nothing was left of the trams except a tangled mass of metal.

"Out of the fog came an old man . . ."

Within two days the tram services in the town were being operated by the neighbouring Bexley system—and Dartford never had its own fleet of trams again.

As fascinating as the stories about ghosts are those concerning mysterious objects in the sky.

A strange phenomenon was witnessed by a tramcar full of people in the first world war.

It happened immediately after a storm on a tram route which ran alongside an electric locomotive test track.

The storm lasted for only minutes on what was otherwise a very calm night. But it was a very fierce and frightening storm, with a heavy downpour of rain and a rush of wind.

As soon as it was over a large "ball" appeared and hovered a few feet above the railway track. It was about the size of an elephant, very bright, like a ball of red-hot metal, showering sparks in all directions.

The driver of the tram pulled up so that all the passengers could see the object. The sight took everybody's breath away, and some passengers gave the sign of the cross, praying that the ball wouldn't start moving in the direction of the tram.

After a minute, the object vanished as quickly as it had appeared. Nobody knew where it went. Nobody knew what it was. It remains a mystery to this day,

This Bolton tram was involved in two collisions in the early years of the war. Here it has collided with another tram on the Cosgrave loop near Tong Moor terminus. Not long afterwards it became the only Bolton tram to fall on its side when it was hit by a runaway tram at Folds Road. After the second accident it had to be rebuilt.

Chapter of accidents

STOP WATCH

Prince Hendrik of the Netherlands accepted full responsibility when his carriage collided with a tramcar. He gave the tram driver a gold watch for promptly stopping his car and averting a more serious accident.

SAFER IN SPACE

First-man-in-space Yuri Gagarin was more at home in sputniks than motorcars. Driving in Moscow, fresh from his triumphant flight, he collided with a tramcar. His fame saved him from the wrath of the tram crew, who changed their abuse to warm smiles and handshakes when they recognised him.

OUTRAGEOUS COLLISION

American president Theodore Roosevelt was bruised, cut and severely shaken, and his bodyguard killed, when a streetcar collided with the landau taking them to a country club at Pittsfield, Massachusetts, in 1902. The president told the horrified motorman: "I think this is the most damnable outrage I ever heard of."

TURN FOR THE WORSE

A coffin turned over when the hearse that was carrying it was involved in a collision with a tramcar. The mourners were very shocked and subsequently succeeded in getting damages in the Liverpool Court of Passage.

ALL AT SEA

A Blackpool lifeboat collided with a trailer tram crowded with holidaymakers. It was being backed out of the boathouse by its tractor when the accident happened. Glass showered into the tram and on to the promenade, but nobody was hurt.

SMASH HIT

Two trams brought out for the official inspection of the new tramway at Batley crashed into each other shortly after leaving the depot.

Good theatre

STAGED AT DEPOTS

Political rallies were held in the Reading tram sheds during 1910. The sheds held some 20,000 people who assembled to hear Lloyd George and Balfour speak. A temporary floor was laid over the pits and it was found that the overhead electric wires improved the accoustics of the sheds. Tramcars conveyed the audience to all parts of the town immediately after the meetings.

In Munich, a tram shed was used as a theatre in 1980 for the presentation of a dramatised documentary "The Charter 77 Trial" by French opera director Patrice Chereau. Among those taking part were the actress Simone Signoret and her husband the actor Yves Montand, and the playwrights Tom Stoppard and Tankred Dorst. The shed seated 840 and the performance was sold out, proceeds going to the families of persecuted Czechoslovakians.

FROM FREEZE TO BREEZE

In the BBC TV thriller series 'Adam Adamant', the character in the title role, who had been in deep freeze since 1895, woke up in 1966 to find himself in a Blackpool tram.

GOT IT TAPED

A tram was used for sound effects in a Radio Three broadcast of 'Julius Caesar'. The BBC said a slowed-down tape of a tram gave a realistic impression of senate doors closing.

TRUNK ROUTE

Elephant rides were among the attractions provided at a Yorkshire amusement park specially built to attract traffic to the Leeds-Wakefield trams. The Lofthouse amusement park, opened by the West Riding Electric Tramways Company in 1908, also boasted an ice-skating rink, maze, dance pavilion, balloon ascents, bandstand, and firework displays. It closed in the first world war, when it became a prisoner-of-war camp.

When he topped the bill in music-halls, famous northern comedian Albert Modley did a tram-driver sketch, putting on a cap and standing behind this effective fold-away tram dash complete with controller handle and cymbol-type bell. Re-enacting the sketch here are his son and granddaughter.

"Could get a grandstand view of the games . . ."

To the match

Football supporters packed on to a Bolton tram bound for Burnden Park, home of Bolton Wanderers. It was the first football special of the 1946-7 season.

As soon as it was full, the car sped off to the ground—but it never got there. The conductor was still busy getting in the fares when the car squealed to a sudden stop at the Technical College.

There was a gap in the track ahead. Somebody had cut away a two-foot length of rail, and the tram could get no further.

A tramway official later explained that during the summer the water department had cut away a section of the track to lay a main. They did not bother to put the rail back because they thought the tram service along Manchester Road had been abandoned.

Regular services past the ground had, in fact, ceased some months before, but the transport department had planned to keep the lines open for Saturday football specials until the end of tramway operations in 1947.

They had to use buses for football specials from that moment onwards—much sooner than they had intended.

The Bolton trams had carried thousands to Burnden Park over the years, especially as the Wanderers were a leading First Division side, attracting large attendances.

In fact, in the early days of the century, councillors often spoke of the crowding of the Manchester Road trams when important matches were held.

"This week I have seen cars so packed there was scarcely room for a mouse," complained one.

Another said that the football cars were so overweighted that their lifeguards kept striking the ground. "I saw 200 on one car, and without a word of exaggeration there were 20 on the bumper bar and steps," he said.

But it was all good business for Bolton Corporation, and for pickpockets, too. About that time a couple of them were caught sharing out their loot among accomplices on the upper deck of a tramcar.

Detectives had watched them jostling among passengers waiting to board cars after a game, and saw them putting their hands in the pockets of unsuspecting fans.

In 1923, Bolton Wanderers met West Ham United in the F.A. Cup Final. That final, the first to be held at Wembley, was memorable because thousands without tickets gatecrashed into the stadium and invaded the pitch, holding up the start of the game until the field was cleared by mounted police.

It was also the occasion West Ham Corporation provided an illuminated tram in honour of the town's team. Glowing with two thousand red, white and blue electric bulbs which said "Well done, Hammers," it toured all the local routes. But it didn't give West Ham the incentive to overcome Bolton Wanderers, who emerged victors 2-0.

Other towns decorated trams to celebrate soccer triumphs, a notable example being the illuminated car which ran in Huddersfield in 1926, when Huddersfield Town won the League Championship for the third year running.

To carry crowds to soccer grounds, tramway operators had to press into service all the spare vehicles they could find. Nearly every major ground in the Football League was on or near a tram route.

In London, for instance, services to rush-hour capacity were run to the capital's eleven League grounds. The LCC tramways provided some 400 cars an hour to and from the Arsenal ground, more than 200 an hour to Millwall and 150 an hour to Tottenham Hotspur.

To encourage football enthusiasts to use the trams, the LCC issued a neat pocket fixture card giving a list of all the principal matches and full instructions on how to reach the grounds. They also issued a colour poster giving the numbers of the appropriate tram routes.

For the Cup finals at Wembley the Metropolitan Electric Tramways ran 50 cars an hour on the Harrow Road, augmenting the special bus and underground services.

In Manchester, 150 special cars were pressed into use for City's games at Maine Road, and in 1926 two cars for "women only" were introduced. They were given a "trial" because women supporters had had difficulty in getting on the ordinary football specials in the homeward rush after matches. But they didn't score a big hit.

To cater for the heavy traffic at large capacity grounds, some tramway operators laid special sidings or tracks in side streets on which to park their trams during a game. Leeds, Huddersfield, Aberdeen and Blackburn were classic examples.

In Birmingham, the tram route passing West Bromwich Albion's ground had four tracks—enabling cars to be parked on either side of the road without interfering with through traffic.

Outside the Birmingham City ground at St. Andrew's, normal service tracks were used for parking, and at match times cars on the 84 route to Stechford via Deritend were diverted over the tracks of route 90 to Stechford via Fazeley Street.

A similar situation prevailed in Scotland at Dens Park, home of Dundee football club. Football specials were parked on service tracks outside the ground and normal service cars were diverted down another street.

Tram enthusiasts Ian Smith and Roy Brook of Huddersfield spent a Saturday afternoon in 1953 watching football cars arriving at Dens Park. They were also able to see how efficiently the St. John Ambulance treated the injuries of drunken supporters who fell off the trams as they arrived at the gates.

The sidings most popular with the crews themselves were probably those in Cherry Street, Sheffield, outside United's ground, for here crews could get a grandstand view of the games from the upper decks of their parked trams.

Special fares were charged on trams bound for matches, and there were special arrangements for fare collection, with some cars carrying additional or roving conductors.

In Dundee, Stockport and one or two other towns, tickets were issued to passengers as they queued on the pavements at main terminuses.

On some systems the special fares were dearer than the ordinary fares. In Nottingham, for instance, they were 2d compared with 1½d. The Nottingham tramways department claimed that little profit was to be gained from running special cars after the costs of extra wages and power had been met.

The receipts received certainly didn't compensate for the damage sometimes inflicted. For there were occasions, such as Cup ties, when seats were slashed and obscene words carved on the interior wooden panelling of cars—and this was before the days of graffiti and paint aerosols.

But football hooligans have been with us a long time. They were causing trouble at the turn of the century, and in 1901 a game between Newcastle

Stretching as far as the eye can see, Birmingham trams line up on the special kerbside tracks provided for football traffic serving The Hawthorns, home of West Bromwich Albion.

and Sunderland was called off because of fighting between rival fans.

At the Centenary Exhibition of Trams in London in 1961, a visitor recalled the time he and other passengers were terrorised by Millwall fans at New Cross.

"They snatched my trilby off me and threw it up and down the upper saloon as if it was a football," he said. "There was nothing I could do about it, and I never saw that hat again, for it rolled down the stairs and fell into the street."

Even when trams were scrapped, some of them continued to have soccer and rugby connections. An old Bradford tram entered retirement as a scoreboard at Odsall stadium, and a Leicester tram was used as a team changing room.

Both these cars have subsequently been restored and are now preserved in museums. The Leicester tram is at the National Tramway Museum at Crich, and its seats still bear marks by boot studs.

Many tramway undertakings had their own football teams, and in Manchester there was one specially for trolley boys.

Alexander Brown of Hinde Street, Moston, recalls playing for the trolley boys between 1922 and 1925 on Hulme Hall recreation ground, near Bradford Road gasworks.

"Sailed straight into a passing tram . . ."

"We played teams from other depots on weekday mornings when we were not on duty. It was great fun, but a lot of pride was at stake," he said.

One January in 1925 the team reached the ground late for a match because subsidence had caused a large hole to appear in Oldham Road, stopping all the trams.

The cavity was about 15ft deep and had been discovered by a policeman who had heard water running and noticed a slight depression in the setts after a car had passed.

Mr. Brown also recalls being struck by lightning while on point duty in Piccadilly. "It flashed all round and I got a shock from the point iron," he told me. "I was very frightened, and waiting passengers said it was a miracle I was still alive. I couldn't leave my post as the trams would have gone down the wrong tracks." Luckily the shock didn't impair his soccer prowess.

The Hulme Hall recreation ground was on Manchester's famous 53 route, and it would be surprising if some passing cars were not hit by miskicked or deflected balls—as happened in Dewsbury when one boy was playing in goal for his school team. The nets were near the road and when he tipped a powerfully-driven ball over the bar it sailed straight into a passing tram.

In 1905, a Municipal Tramway Football League was formed. It was affiliated to the Football Association and its first members were Manchester, Sheffield, Wigan, Southport and Liverpool.

Sheffield were the first champions, winning the Challenge Trophy with 13 points from eight games.

"The Sheffield tramways department is to be congratulated on possessing such an excellent team, which on last season's form will be difficult to beat," said the Tramway League secretary in his first report.

Sheffield tramways, like a number of other undertakings, later had its own football ground for employees.

If every news story printed in the newspapers is to be believed, then it seems there were also football matches for trams.

One newspaper published a news item which said: "Football League clubs will consider participating in a floodlit competition starting next season, embracing English, Scottish, Irish and Welsh trams."

Now that really would have been something to see. It was a misprint, of course, like the "improved pram services to Old Trafford" that a Manchester newspaper once reported.

Adventures

Our journeys all adventures were
When we to Trawden went by car,
We'd long been used to sways and swerves,
Which rudely shook and jabbed our nerves.
But now the men with pick and spade
The wobbly places have relaid;
Henceforth the trams will glide, not jar,
Thanks to the men with sand and tar.

—Anon

The end of the line for Manchester's trams on 10 July, 1949, as the last car enters Birchfields Road depot. Now Manchester is obtaining powers to run trams again, but their new cars will look more like the Nantes vehicle on page 123 than the one above.

End of the line

TRAM CHIEF'S DEATH

Sir James Clifton Robinson, general manager of the London United Tramways, died on board a New York streetcar shortly after retiring in 1910.

ENGULFED

Three fully-laden New York streetcars were engulfed and many persons killed and injured when 150 yards of road collapsed during excavations of a subway in 1915.

MURDER SPECIALS

Special trams were laid on to the "Murder Caves" in Johannesburg during August and September 1914. The caves, near a tram route, became a sightseeing attraction after a criminal surrounded by police murdered his family in them before committing suicide.

KILLED BY PITCHFORK

When Home Rule rioters attacked a horse tram depot in Belfast in 1886, one of them was killed by a pitchfork wielded by a tramway worker in self defence.

HORRIFIC START

A five-year-old boy watching the start of electric trams in the Potteries ran into the path of one of the first trams and was killed.

FATAL BLAST

The boiler of a Bury steam tram exploded in 1898 just after the tram had returned to the depot, killing a cleaner and hurling the tram engine across the depot yard.

An oxygen cylinder wrecked a Greenock tramcar and damaged another in 1924 when it exploded after falling off a steam lorry which was being unloaded outside the Dockyard store in Main Street. The blast injured 40 people, many of them being cut in the face by glass, and two passengers were blown downstairs.

Clean round the bend

BLACKLEADED LINES

Tram lines were hand-polished at Hazel Grove (near Stockport), Tottington (near Bury) and Zagreb in Yugoslavia. The custom was started at Hazel Grove when a practical joker convinced residents that under the Tramways Act they had to clean the lines outside their houses, otherwise they would be pulled up. The "Grovers" swallowed the tale, and got up early to polish the lines with brushes and blacklead.

SEAT SPONGERS

On the steam trams running between Manchester, Bury, Rochdale and Oldham conductors carried cotton waste and a piece of sponge cloth to keep the seats clean.

ON REFLECTION

A full-length mirror was placed in a prominent position in the Southend-on-Sea tram sheds, with printed instructions that drivers and conductors should have well-brushed cap and clothes, polished boots and buttons, a good shave and pressed trousers.

A TONIC

At the turn of the century it was claimed that trams were beneficial to health because they "produced ozone which purified the atmosphere and killed off germs." The ozone was produced by the "great quantities of electricity discharged from overhead wires and tram wheels."

TERMINAL SPRAY

During an influenza epidemic at Chester in 1927 trams were sprayed with disinfectant at the end of each journey because passengers complained it was too draughty with the windows open.

SOILED

Bolton tramcar No. 66 and its driver had to have a special bath in the thirties after being in collision with a night soil truck, which tipped up and deposited all its contents on the car's front platform.

Modern washing plant at Glasgow's Parkhead depot kept the city's famous Coronation class trams in sparkling condition.

Blackleading the tram lines at Hazel Grove (previously known as Bullock Smithy) as pictured on an early comic postcard. It is also rumoured that the village put up wire netting to keep out chicken pox.

Brief delight

"Sometines the cable watchers go mad with the endless monotony of their work, because when you have watched a cable for a year you will watch a cable in your mind for the rest of your life."

—The Guardian, writing about San Francisco cable cars

"What more awe-inspiring symbol of progress could there have been for the coming twentieth century than a vast tramcar ablaze with the new electric light and piloted by a bearded genie whirling polished brass handles, and from time to time stepping imperiously on a pedal which rang a sonorous gong to clear the path of progress?"

—The Engineer

"It's a funny thing about trams. Like artichokes and the Marx Brothers, you either esteem them very highly or not at all."

—Evening News, London

"Trams didn't have the intimidating class divisions of trains. Trams were for the people to cram into, to sing in and laugh in. A tram was a transport of brief delight. You didn't meet the boss in it. Trams blossomed wherever there were people, multiplying in the jabbering crowds like lizards in the undergrowth. They vanished from Britain while people were looking up at the new skyscrapers and counting their overtime money."

—Granada TV

"Have you ever tried moving a tramcar? You need a lot of ingenuity, a lot of patience, and (worst of all) a lot of money. You cannot just tow it down the road; you leave two furrows and get a rude letter from the council. You cannot mark it marchandise roulante and send it in a goods train; it would derail at the first curve."

—John Price, President, National Tramway Museum

"Pedalled furiously up to his car . . ."

From pillar to post

When a woman accidentally posted her wedding ring in Coventry she had to get on her bicycle and chase the post-box.

The post-box was attached to a tram, and the incident is recalled by Henry Wilkinson, a Coventry tram conductor from 1934 until 1939.

He was working on the Bedworth service when the woman pedalled furiously up to his car. Gasping for breath she explained to him that when she had posted her letter at the previous stop she had also posted her wedding ring, which had slipped from her finger.

"I told her that I didn't have a key to the box," said Mr. Wilkinson. "But I advised her to get on her bike and ride to the city centre and with luck she would be able to get the postman to return her ring. She reached the city terminus at the same time as the tram, looking hot and bothered."

Mr. Wilkinson told the postman what had happened and the lady went with him to the nearby sorting office where the box was opened and the ring returned.

The postal service on Coventry tramcars started on 6 July, 1925, the

A Manchester post car. One car like this ran on each of Manchester's tram routes every night before the second world war, leaving outer terminuses at nine o'clock.

boxes being provided on trams leaving Bedworth at 9.24 p.m. and Bell Green at 9.30 p.m. The words "Postal car" were displayed in red on the route indicator.

"It was a useful service to the public, but keeping to schedule on these journeys was sometimes difficult, especially on Thursday nights, when there were people waiting at every stop to post their football coupons," added Mr. Wilkinson.

At Liverpool, another city where trams carried post-boxes, four postmen were on duty at the Pier Head to collect the late night post. They took about 5,000 letters and cards out of 30 trams as they came in at about 10.30 p.m.

One of the postmen said: "It was a tough job making the collection. We had to run round all the terminal stops emptying the boxes, and at the same time pick up mail from the ferries coming across from the Wirral. But once we had done the job and got the mail back to the office we were off duty, so you can imagine how fast we were."

Liverpool started its tramcar postal service in 1925 with boxes on one evening car on four routes and extended the service four months later.

Tramcar postal services were provided in about 30 cities and towns in Britain, but in most cases they were confined to certain cars at specific hours only, giving outlying suburbs a late night collection after the last collection from street boxes.

In Huddersfield, however, a more extensive service was provided, post boxes being fixed to all cars throughout the day.

The service in Huddersfield was the first in the country. It started on the steam trams on 20 March, 1893. No preliminary announcement was made, yet despite this there were 13 letters in the first boxes cleared.

By the end of the day more than 500 letters had been posted, and the total collected from 28 steam trams in the first week was 4,000.

The boxes were cleared every hour from 8.30 a.m. until 9.30 p.m., with a final clearance at 11 p.m. Letters cleared at 8.30 p.m. were in time for the London, Midland, Scottish and Irish mails. Letters posted earlier in the day and addressed to premises in the centre of the town were delivered within an hour or two.

The boxes, designed by the tramways manager and postal authorities, were fastened to the rear of each passenger car by an automatic spring lock.

The number of letters carried at Huddersfield had risen to 33,000 a month by 1897, to 50,000 a month in 1903, after electrification of the tramways, and to 85,000 in 1927, although the last collection was then 8 p.m.

The success of the Huddersfield service encouraged five other tramway operators to start carrying post-boxes later in 1892. These were at Bradford, Dublin, Portsmouth, Stockport and Wakefield. But only at Stockport were the results worthwhile.

The four boxes on the horse cars of the Stockport and Hazel Grove

Carriage Company took 6,250 letters in the first week, compared with only 780 letters from 22 boxes on Portsmouth trams.

The service lasted until 1905, and one Hazel Grover said that she remembers her mother ordering her father to chase the tram in his clogs one night to post an urgent letter which she wanted to reach her sister in Hyde the next day.

Other tramways which followed Huddersfield's example in providing post-boxes on its cars included Bexley, Birkenhead, Blackpool, Bradford, Camborne and Redruth, Cleethorpes, Coventry, Croydon, Dewsbury, Dundee, Great Yarmouth, Halifax, Hull, Ilford, Kirkcaldy, Leeds, Liverpool, Manchester, Northampton, Nottingham, Notts and Derby, Rhondda, Rochdale, Rotherham, Salford, Sheffield, Southampton, Southport, Sunderland, Sunderland District, Swansea, Walsall, Warwick and Wigan.

On most of these systems, boxes made just one journey a day on late cars, while at Bexley the Council charged a penny every time the car was specially stopped.

On the Ilford system, collections were bedevilled for a short while by a practical joker who kept dropping objectionable items in the boxes.

At Wakefield the service was abandoned in 1904 when the tramways company demanded a halfpenny for each letter posted on the cars.

Some authorities wouldn't entertain the idea of having post-boxes fixed to their trams. They claimed that posting a letter in a busy street could be dangerous and that it caused delays to the trams.

The postmasters in some towns also were not keen on the idea. They said the cost involved in supplying boxes and emptying them at terminuses was higher than the cost for street boxes and they didn't see any justification for the expenditure.

Newcastle upon Tyne and Glasgow tramways were not interested because their cars did not converge on one central point near a sorting office. "The cost of collection would be heavy and out of all proportion to any benefit to be derived," said a spokesman for Newcastle.

The tramway operators at Belfast, Bolton, Bristol and Oldham were opposed to carrying boxes in any circumstances. "If the matter were pressed, we would impose such conditions that the scheme would be rendered absolutely impracticable," said a Belfast official.

It was quite the reverse at Sheffield, where the Corporation was anxious for post-boxes to be carried in order to popularise the tram services.

At Lincoln the project was not adopted because the tramways department refused to give an indemnity against accidents to members of the public endeavouring to post letters on moving tramcars.

There were some people, in fact, who found it difficult enough to post a letter while the car was stopped. A woman writing about the tramcar postal services in Amsterdam, which lasted until recent years, said: "Every time

I reached the tram and stretched out my hand to post the letter, the tram sailed away. My friends on the pavement were in convulsions."

Before the first world war, most major American towns ran trolley mail cars. Painted white, they carried mail between the main post offices and railway stations, and had facilities aboard which enabled clerks to sort out and frank mail as the cars sped along the street tracks.

It is a pity that all the letters and cards posted on town tramcar services were not specially franked, as are letters posted at sea. With the rapidly-growing interest in postmarks, they would have been valuable today, especially if they had included slogans like "Walk wearily, Tram cheerily," which at one time was franked on Edinburgh Transport Department's outgoing letters, or "Don't leave your journey home to the last bus or tram; it might be full!" which was franked on Manchester tramways' envelopes.

T for tramway

T stands for Tramway, I speak it with awe,
Such a well conceived project the world never saw,
The clean gorgeous cars are propelled by a power,
Which relentlessly drives them at three miles an hour.

—Anon

The midnight caur

There were tipsy blokes sae happy,
Bawlin' out 'Sweet Adeline',
There were lovers in the corner
Thinkin' everything was fine.
An' some folk tae see a sodger aff
Who sang 'For Auld Lang Syne',
On the dear auld midnight caur.

It usually was crooded out,
Wi' passengers a roar'n,
An' mony saw it flyin' past
When rain was steady pour'n,
But now it disnae rin at a',
An' mony mair'll mourn
The passing o' th' midnight caur.

—Anon

Only a fortnight before he was killed in an air crash, Prince William, Duke of Gloucester, drives a tram at the National Tramway Museum at Crich in Derbyshire. His instructor (left) is Roger Benton of Sheffield.

Reel treats

In the dead of night some shady New York characters in the employ of a devious trolley car magnate steal a horse tram.

It is the last horse tram in the city, running every day over lines that thc trolley car magnate would dearly love to acquire at rock-bottom price and electrify.

All the owner of the horse car has to do to resist the take-over and keep his franchise is provide a daily service.

The thieves hide the horse tram on a derelict site on the other side of the city.

Things look black for the horse car's owner, but he has a staunch ally—his daughter's suitor, Harold Lloyd.

Harold tracks down the car, rescues it, and at high speed drives it back to its home with the thieves in hot pursuit.

On the way, he crashes the tram against a pillar, smashing one of the wheels.

Not to be outdone, Harold replaces it with a manhole cover, and arrives back, just in the nick of time, of course.

The sequences occur in "Speedy," Harold Lloyd's last silent film made in 1928.

A copy of the film is held by the National Tramway Museum at Crich in Derbyshire in its unique library of tramway films.

The library, the most comprehensive of its kind in the world, contains more than 300 films assembled over a period of 15 years mainly through the efforts of Roger Benton of Sheffield.

Said Roger: "The films are a very valuable source of reference for the social historian, but they are also good entertainment."

"Speedy," needless to say, is one of his favourite films. Another is "Down Market Street," a 12-minute film taken in San Francisco in 1905 before the earthquake.

The cine photographer tied his camera to the front of one of the city's famous cable cars and then took a run down the whole length of Market Street, which is the city's most famous thoroughfare.

"I see something different in the film every time I show it, there's so much action going on in the street," said Roger.

As curator of the film archives, Roger spends half his holidays showing the films to different tramway and railway societies up and down the country.

The films portray trams of all kinds running in cities all over the world—from Shanghai to Mexico City.

They include first and last trams, trams in chases, trams demonstrating road safety, trams driven by royalty, trams ploughing through floods and struggling through snow.

They even feature the Red Devils. But these Red Devils are firmly planted on the ground. They are the big red cars of the Cincinnati and Lake Erie interurban line, which clocked 90 mph during their trials in 1930 and left police motorcyclists behind.

The film, shot in 1934, includes a race between one of the Red Devils and a Jenny bi-plane. The aeroplane is soundly beaten.

Royal occasions captured on celluloid include King Edward VII and Queen Alexandra disembarking from a steamboat at Greenwich Pier in 1905 and boarding a decorated white tram.

A more recent film, taken in 1976, shows King Edward's great grandson, Prince Richard, Duke of Gloucester, first royal patron of the National Tramway Museum, driving one of the trams at Crich.

When the Duke's late brother, Prince William, also visited the museum on 14 August, 1972, it fell to Roger to show him how to handle the controls of a tram.

One of the oldest films shows horse, steam and electric trams running together in Boar Lane, Leeds, in 1903.

There is also rare film, taken later in his life, of Michael Holroyd Smith, the engineer who opened Britain's first electric tramway system at Blackpool in 1885, and, uniquely, there is in the collection a short sequence showing his conduit cars in action in 1899.

To delight young and old Roger has tracked down some cartoon films of trams, including the Toonerville Trolley.

Toonerville gets stuck in quicksands and is attacked by a runaway bull in one six-minute film. In another, the driver ties a sail on Toonerville when the power fails and all goes well until a tornado catches it.

There is little doubt, however, that the most entertaining films in the Crich archives are those featuring Harold Lloyd, who drew more humour from trams than any other film comedian, including Charlie Chaplin, whose only contribution appears to be "Pay Day," in which he is thwarted from boarding a car.

In "Girl Shy" Harold finds himself clinging desperately to a trolley pole

Filming for the TV programme "Nationwide" at the National Tramway Museum in 1977, with Tom Coyne at the controls of a Johannesburg tram. The programme extolled the virtues of the tram and showed the work that is put into tramcar preservation by enthusiasts. The museum's trams also regularly star in films for the cinema and television drama and comedy programmes.

swinging out from a runaway car. In another film a turkey he has won in a raffle causes him no end of trouble when he takes it home on a trolley car.

Even alighting and boarding can present Harold with tricky situations that few passengers in a lifetime of travelling would ever have thought possible.

The films in the archives have come from various sources—some from tram lovers, others from authorities and film companies.

A dozen reels of Birmingham trams in the twenties were discovered rotting in a garden shed in the West of England and rescued before the images on them had faded completely.

A film of West Ham trams in 1925 was discovered in a Mansfield antique shop. Other valuable films found in the shop at the same time have since gone to the British Film Institute.

Some of the more recent sound films in the Crich archives have come from British television services. They are copies of programmes made by the BBC and independent channels on the museum's trams.

They include "I Didn't Know You Cared" (1977); "We're Going Places" (1980); "Blue Peter" (1983); "Yesterday's World;" and "Shabby Tiger," Granada TV's serial of Howard Spring's novel set in Manchester.

"Yesterday's World" was a special Christmas edition of "Tomorrow's World," with Raymond Baxter road testing an open balcony tram on the museum's lines.

In 1975, Yorkshire Television made a film of the Tramway Museum in which Roger was interviewed.

"It never occurred to me that when I started this film collection I would be pictured in it myself," he joked.

The tram museum has also been used for big cinema productions, like "Women in Love" and "Secret Places."

For "Secret Places," which is about a German schoolgirl interned in England during the last war, the trams had to be converted to wartime appearance, with white fenders, blast netting on the windows and masks on the headlamps.

Providing facilities such as these for film companies and television has earned the National Tramway Museum valuable income since it was established in 1959.

Previously, film producers had to use trams still in regular service on city streets, as they did, for example, in Belfast for "Odd Man Out" and in Liverpool for "Waterfront."

Few of the early film makers, however, chose Manchester for their location work while the city still had trams. It's an ommission that Roger finds regrettable.

"Just think of all the trams that once ran in Manchester," he said. "There were hundreds of them, and yet our collection has barely five minutes on Manchester, compared with three hours at least on both Glasgow and Birmingham and well over an hour each on London, Leeds and Sheffield."

Preserve us

"Mama! Mama! What is that mess that looks like strawberry jam?"
"Hush, hush, my child; it is papa run over by a tram."

—Anon

Ah! This was how we learnt life's golden rule,
To swallow bitter pills without the jam,
In this the most progressive public school,
This mobile university—the tram!

—Bolton tram driver

O! the tram, the Portstewart tram;
How the doors close with a vigorous slam;
How the fish boxes are packed in the van;
With the mails and the papers and the morning milk-can
And sausages, butter, eggs, bacon and ham;
All bundled together in glorious conglam.

—Anon

In the three rear pews
You may smoke if you choose;
'Tis the rule of the open car.
But you'll hear, I'm afraid,
Some fussy old maid
Say "Oh, that horrid seegar!"

—Anon

Burning issues

BLAZING SUPPORT

A figure was left hanging from the overhead wires on Melbourne's first tramway for a whole week in 1891 before being tossed into a roaring pitch fire by a crowd of 800 tramway supporters. The figure was a stuffed dummy replica of a land agent who had stopped the tram service by chopping down poles carrying wires across his land. The crowd held a mock service and gave three hearty jeers.

SET ON FIRE

Armed men stopped a Belfast tramcar in 1922, saturated it with paraffin and after setting it on fire sent it running towards the city centre. It ran for half a mile before someone was able to pull the trolley pole off the overhead wires. Residents then extinguished the flames.

In the burning of Cork in December, 1920, a tramcar (No. 3) was set on fire by police and auxiliaries after they had ordered off and searched the passengers.

TERRIBLE END

A woman was burnt to death while riding on the top deck of a Dublin tram taking her to see a review of the troops. She was sitting on a single seat when, suddenly, her dress burst into flames. Before any of the other passengers could save her she suffered terrible burns, from which she died shortly afterwards. It was presumed her dress was set alight by a thrown-away cigarette end.

IN THE FIRING LINE

In 1964, 11 Calcutta tramcars were set on fire after violence erupted following the arrest of a passenger who had not paid his fare. In the same city in 1953, demonstrators set 13 trams on fire in protest against fare increases.

STRIKE A LIGHT

For striking a match against the newly-painted side of a Bolton tramcar in 1908 a man was fined one shilling with costs. For committing a similar offence at Mansfield in 1923, a man was fined 10s 6d, with 13s 9d damages; he had struck several other matches when told off by the conductor.

"Left hanging for a whole week . . ."

Between the lines

PUNCH LINE

Hamburg tramways provided reading matter for its passengers and Punch and Judy shows for local school children.

ON HONEYMOON

In 1904, an American travelled 500 miles by trolley car on his honeymoon. He took his bride from Wilmington, Delaware, to York Beach, Maine, travelling on the streetcars of different systems.

ODDS OR EVENS

In Portsmouth, tram services were double numbered—odd for inwards and even for outwards.

OFF THE RAILS

A "moonlight flit" by the horse tramways company at South Shields in 1886 left the town tramless for a year. The company drove their six cars to the end of the lines at Tyne Dock and dragged them to a yard a mile away, where they were stored until bought by Douglas Corporation. No explanation was given to the astonished travelling public. A new company restarted services in 1887.

TIME CAPSULE

Among the items included in a time capsule concreted in the Bowes-Lyon Bridge at the National Tramway Museum in 1984 were tram tickets, timetables, a tram driver's licence and a certificate of tram riding.

DELAYED BY BALLOON

A barrage balloon delayed trams on Stockport's Cheadle Heath service during the second world war. Its trailing cable damaged some overhead wires at Cheadle Heath station after it had broken away from its moorings.

STOP PRESS

Bolton trams were used throughout their life for the daily delivery of the Bolton Evening News.

Bringing the trams back. This sleek car, holding 168 passengers, graces the streets of Nantes—one of the many towns throughout the world now re-introducing tram services. The lines are laid entirely on segregated rights-of-way and the French government paid half the construction costs. Cars can reach speeds up to 70 kilometres an hour. The system opened on 7 January, 1985.

Modern light rail vehicles made by Boeing running on segregated right-of-way in Boston, one American city that long ago placed its faith in modern trams.

Acknowledgments

Grateful thanks to those listed below for kindly supplying photographs:

Boeing Vertol, America 124; Bolton Evening News 54,80, 94; Harold Brearley 75; British Gas North Western 49; the late Wilfred Burrows 29; W. A. Camwell 101; Daily Express 17, 68; Detroit Department of Public Information 59; Harry Dibdin 79; Alan Dixon 26 (bottom); David Frodsham 117; Harry Furness 97; Glasgow Corporation Transport 107 (top); Halifax Building Society 14; S. Holt/GMPTE 123; D. W. K. Jones 110; Walter McGrath 85 (top); Manchester Polytechnic Faculty of Community Studies 43 (bottom); National Tramway Museum 114; Peter Oldham 26 (top); Southern Newspapers frontispiece; Weekend 85 (bottom).

Subscribers

D. L. G. Adeley, Bristol
W. Aitken, Edinburgh
F. A. Allen, Hadleigh, Essex
D. Allinson, Darlington
A. Askew, London

N. Bailes, Salford
J. P. Bainton, Hereford
J. Baldwin, Sale
Dr. P. Banister, Oldham
J. M. Barber, Wrexham
H. Barnett, Holloway, Derbyshire
A. F. Barrett, Peebles
D. M. Barwell, Droitwich
Rev. P. M. Battersby, Hull
Mrs. B. Baxter, Meltham
D. T. Beach, Newbury
A. Beaumont, Huddersfield
C. Beaumont, Linthwaite
D. M. Beardsell, West Bridgford
F. J. Beckley, Ashford, Kent
H. E. Bellamy, Leicester
S. Beresford, Buxton
A. J. Bertram, Ilford
Mrs. A. V. Bigwood, Lee, London
C. Billington, Huddersfield
Bournemouth Transport Museum
R. Briers, Coventry
A. Broady, Cheadle Hulme
R. Brook, Huddersfield
J. C. Brown, Wolverhampton

W. A. Camwell, Birmingham
P. J. Cardno, Stockton-on-Tees
P. J. Carr, Sawbridgeworth
B. C. Castle, Cirencester
B. Cavell, Leeds
K. Chadbourne, Manchester
F. Charlton, Sunderland
M. Chisholm, Southport
M. J. Chiswick, Nottingham
R. J. Clarke, Chiswick
G. B. Claydon, West Kensington
P. S. Cliff, Ilkley
N. D. Cocker, Heald Green
N. Cockle, Oban
M. G. Collignon, Quinton
M. J. Collinson, Leeds
S. Cooke, Sheffield
C. M. Cooksey, Horley, Surrey
B. O. Cooper, Leicester
F. W. Cooper, Tuckenhay
Mrs. M. Cormack, Cambuslang
A. W. Cornish, London
D. W. Cowe, Ravenshead
M. C. Crabtree, Doncaster
D. J. Croft, Bradford
R. Crombleholme, Birmingham
B. J. Cross, Croydon
W. S. Cunningham, Rossett
P. R. Curzon, Gillingham

E. W. Dash, Southampton
R. J. Dawson, London
R. W. Deacon, Blackboys
W. E. Deamer, Lee Green, London
D. J. Dean, Bean
B. W. Decker, Welwyn Garden City
R. Delahoy, Thorpe Bay
Rev. A. E. Dixon, Huddersfield
E. Dodgson, Blaydon
E. N. Doe, Chesham

V. L. Dominy, Hampton, Middlesex
D. W. Doolin, Alderley Edge
I. M. Dougill, Leeds
R. P. Drew, Great Sankey
C. D. Drewe, Chelmsford
C. S. Dunbar, Malvern
G. R. Dunning, Manchester

B. Eaton, Camberley
B. Edison, London
I. Edwards, Liverpool
P. Elliott, Leicester
D. G. Evans, Bexleyheath
D. R. Evans, Blackpool
A. M. Eyre, Glossop

F. K. Farrell, Addlestone
G. A. Feakins, Dulwich
D. F. Felton, Birmingham
R. K. Fenelon, Paris
L. W. Field, Bromley
G. Firth, Harlow
L. Forshaw, Ormskirk
A. G. Forsyth, East Barnet
A. L. Foulner, York
D. F. M. Fraser, Croydon
Dr. I. D. O. Frew, Sutton Coldfield
D. Frodsham, Wood Green

J. Garnham, Blackpool
P. F. Gavin, Worsley
R. Gee, Sidcup
J. B. Gent, South Croydon
E. A. Gildersleve, East Dulwich
Miss A. D. Gill, Stockport
G. & B. Gill, Chapel-en-le-Frith
Miss K. L. Gill, Stockport
R. M. Gillespie, Welling
D. Gooch, Bristol
J. K. Goodwin, Hull
R. Goodwin, Northampton
T. Goulding, Bolton
S. Gow, Alva, Clacks
B. Graham, Leytonstone
E. Gray, Salford
A. H. Green, Teddington
R. P. Green, Folkestone
Mrs. Y. Gregitis, Blackpool
G. Guilmartin, Galashiels

M. Hague, Rotherham
J. F. Haigh, Halifax
D. Hale, South Ruislip
V. H. Hale, Brighton
H. G. Hall, Blaenau Ffestiniog
B. R. Hallett, Derby
P. R. Hand, Stockport
M. G. Hardwick, Carshalton Beeches
R. J. Harley, Hailsham
D. D. H. Harper, Oundle
N. H. Harper, Croydon
J. W. Harpur, Ambergate
J. A. Harrison, Leeds
D. J. Haynes, Macclesfield
E. N. C. Haywood, Rawtenstall
W. S. Heaton, Flixton
R. E. Heaven, St. Saviour, Jersey
R. Heginbotham, Stockport
S. M. Hemingway, Selby
R. A. Henton, St. Helens
E. Hepworth, Telscombe Cliffs
R. Herriott, Luton
Mrs. S. Hilditch, Doncaster
Mrs. B. Hill, Stoney Middleton
R. Hill, Altrincham
G. N. Hindley, Keighley
D. W. Hitchen, Gloucester
L. E. Hodges, Maidenhead
G. Hodgson, Kirkburton
J. K. Holdsworth, Huddersfield
D. C. G. Holt, Davyhulme
N. A. Holt, Aintree
B. M. K. Horner, York
Dr. J. B. Howard, Kegworth
M. Howard, Newcastle upon Tyne
J. Howe, Romford
R. A. Howse, Winchester
E. Hudson, Blackpool
R. H. Hughes, Altrincham
E. Humphreys, London
A. Hunt, Stretford
A. P. Huntingford, Barnet
H. A. Hurst, Poulton-le-Fylde
Dr. S. A. Hutchinson, Slough

G. T. Ingall, Longdon, Tewkesbury
C. F. Isgar, West Drayton

E. Jackson-Stevens, Glastonbury
A. E. D. James, Wareham
D. Jones, Kentish Town
K. Jones, Aberdeen
P. A. Jones, Wimborne

R. S. Jones, Wallasey
F. R. Johnson, Rhos-on-Sea
G. B. Johnston, Aberdeen
H. E. Jordan, Reading

J. A. Kelso, Wolverhampton
N. G. P. Kibby, Yeovil
J. S. King, Bradford
W. J. King, Shenstone, Staffs
R. Kirby, West Bridgford
J. W. Klepper, Walthamstow
D. J. Kyle, Market Harborough

K. Lack, Cirencester
L. G. Lambley, Broxbourne
N. Landau, Stockport
R. B. Law, Bicknacre
W. R. Lawrence, St. Peter Port, Guernsey
C. B. Lees, Airdrie
A. J. Lefever, Potters Bar
G. Leigh, Bethesda, Gwynedd
C. J. Lent, Wednesfield
P. Lepino, Great Bookham
C. S. Leslie, Penicuik
S. E. Letts, Oldbury, West Midlands
V. Linden, Blackpool
A. H. Lindley, Manchester
K. Linnett, Bognor Regis
J. R. Little, Bamber Bridge
G. P. Lomas, Sale
R. Lomas, Stillington, York
R. T. Long, Chulmleigh
B. M. Longworth, Scotstoun, Glasgow
I. J. Longworth, Clayton-le-Woods
H. Luff, London
W. Luty, Pudsey

R. F. Mack, Leeds
N. D. G. Mackenzie, Edinburgh
Dr. N. A. MacKillop, Glasgow
E. McCormick, Eccleston, St. Helens
E. P. McCormick, Surbiton
D. W. McEwen, Hazel Grove
A. R. Magenis, Cheam
R. G. Manders, Burnley
J. D. Markham, Stockport
B. W. Marriott, Leicester
J. D. Marsh, Pinner
D. Marshall, Rugby
E. P. Marshall, Sheffield
B. P. Martin, Huyton
R. Meadowcroft, Darwen
D. Mercer, Bromley
W. F. Michell, Southgate, London
J. Miller, Manchester
Rev. J. E. Minor, Warrington
E. J. Minte, Bladon, Oxford
M. Mogford, London
J. R. Moore, Halifax
R. F. Morgan, Cheltenham
A. G. Morris, Altrincham
P. J. Mullahy, Leicester
G. F. C. Munday, Streatham
R. J. Murphy, Tooting, London
A. G. Murray, West Byfleet
D. Murray, Bury
M. Murray, Sunderland

G. L. Newcombe, Goff's Oak
R. W. Newman, London
Dr. P. D. Niblett, Newport, Gwent
J. Nicholls, Blackpool
J. B. Norris, Burgess Hill
H. L. Nuttall, Wye, Kent

G. Oakley, Penrhyn Bay
S. Oliver, Finchley
R. D. Owen, St. Asaph

A. D. Packer, Bickley
G. S. Palmer, York
J. G. Parkinson, Southport
T. Parkinson, Vancouver
B. Percy, Egham
J. Perkins, Edgbaston
M. Petch, Southampton
D. Phipps, West Bromwich
A. G. Piette, Brussells
K. W. Pinnock, Hull
E. N. Pounder, Birmingham

H. P. Preston, Keighley
J. Preston, Lowestoft
G. W. Price, Carnforth
J. H. Price, Peterborough
R. V. Price, Edgbaston
Rev. E. W. Pugh, Liverpool

C. J. Ratcliffe, Halifax
N. Rayfield, London

C. S. Rayner, Enfield
H. Rhodes, Hanley
F. P. Roberts, Sale
B. Robinson, Lancaster
G. P. C. Robinson, Billericay
P. Robinson, Royston, Herts
P. Rogers, Redditch
Colonel D. W. Ronald, Andover
R. G. Rowley, Hornchurch
M. J. Russell, Reading
B. S. Rutter, Curraghroe, Ireland
P. A. Ryan, Warrington

G. Sandford, Billinge
J. Saunders, Atherton
M. Searle, Bracknell
R. Senior, Sheffield
G. Shaw, Hyde
J. Shearer, Blackpool
T. Shorrocks, Stockport
J. Simmons, Weymouth
D. J. Simpson, Bletchley
P. F. Simpson, Battersea
P. Skelton, Retford
E. T. Smith, Leeds
J. Smith, Richmond, Surrey
K. H. Smith, Llandudno
L. N. Smith, Ratho
C. G. Smyth, Knutsford
I. A. Souter, Bridge of Allan
A. R. Spencer, Erdington
R. F. Spencer, Cardiff
G. Spink, Leeds
F. J. F. Stainer, Gosport
W. A. Stearn, Ventnor
K. Stephens, Westcliff-on-Sea
A. Stevenson, St. Annes
R. M. Stevenson, Edinburgh
G. Stoakes, Ilford
J. F. Storey, Runwell
N. Stranaghan, Bangor, N. Ireland
C. Stringer, Stalybridge
L. D. Styles, Birmingham
R. A. Sykes, Oxted

P. H. Tangye, Whitstable
D. Taylor, Retford
R. M. Taylor, Oldham
G. Teasdill, Bournemouth
Dr. R. G. P. Tebb, Wakefield
A. K. Terry, Leeds
C. G. Thompson, Plymouth
T. P. N. Thompson, Uxbridge
D. L. Thomson, Gourock
C. C. Thornburn, Erdington
Mrs. D. E. Thornburn, Leeds
B. H. Thornley, Higher Bebington
B. Thornton, Bebington
D. W. Thornton, Newcastle upon Tyne
W. Tollan, Clarkston
G. C. Train, Edinburgh
G. Turnbull, Higher Irlam

S. H. Urquhart, Manchester

E. R. Vaughan, Liverpool
F. J. Vescoe, Tilford
D. Voice, Kidderminster

A. H. Wadsworth, Blackpool
C. S. N. Walker, Cheltenham
J. S. Walker, Clapham
G. H. Wallis, Clacton
K. N. Walton, Bristol
A. F. Wardle, Newcastle upon Tyne
F. Watson, Wallsend
F. F. Watson, Bradford
D. Watts, Cirencester
H. G. Weaver, Thornton Cleveleys
J. Weeks, South Woodham Ferrers
A. J. Weise, Woking
A. G. Wells, Maidstone
E. Wharmby, New Mills
E. Wheatley, Pudsey
E. J. White, Haywards Heath
A. F. Whitehouse, Oldbury, West Midlands
T. A. Wiles, Warrington
E. I. Williams, Leeds
H. Williams, Penmaenmawr
J. Willshire, Portsmouth
E. Wilson, Hartlepool
R. Wilson, Sheffield
C. M. Wiseman, Owosso, Michigan
B. Wood, Waterlooville
J. Woodman, Harrow
F. A. Woodrow, Muswell Hill
P. D. Worthington, Manchester
E. H. Wrigley, Oldham

D. H. Yarnell, Lincoln
B. L. Yates, Lancaster
I. A. Yearsley, London
W. S. Youngs, Shoeburyness